THE LITTLE BOOK

OF

BIG DIVIDENDS

WITHDRAWN

Little Book Big Profits Series

In the Little Book Big Profits series, the brightest icons in the financial world write on topics that range from tried-and-true investment strategies to tomorrow's new trends. Each book offers a unique perspective on investing, allowing the reader to pick and choose from the very best in investment advice today.

Books in the *Little Book Big Profits* series include:

The Little Book That Beats the Market, in which Joel Greenblatt, founder and managing partner at Gotham Capital, reveals a "magic formula" that is easy to use and makes buying good companies at bargain prices automatic, enabling you to successfully beat the market and professional managers by a wide margin.

The Little Book of Value Investing, in which Christopher Browne, managing director of Tweedy, Browne Company, LLC, the oldest value investing firm on Wall Street, simply and succinctly explains how value investing, one of the most effective investment strategies ever created, works, and shows you how it can be applied globally.

The Little Book of Common Sense Investing, in which Vanguard Group founder John C. Bogle shares his own time-tested philosophies, lessons, and personal anecdotes to explain why outperforming the market is an investor illusion, and how the simplest of investment strategies—indexing—can deliver the greatest return to the greatest number of investors.

The Little Book That Makes You Rich, in which Louis Navellier, financial analyst and editor of investment newsletters since 1980, offers readers a fundamental understanding of how to get rich using the best in growth-investing strategies. Filled with in-depth insights and practical advice, *The Little Book That Makes You Rich* outlines an effective approach to building true wealth in today's markets.

The Little Book That Builds Wealth, in which Pat Dorsey, director of stock analysis for leading independent investment research provider Morningstar, Inc., guides the reader in understanding "economic moats," learning how to measure them against one another, and selecting the best companies for the very best returns.

The Little Book That Saves Your Assets, in which David M. Darst, a managing director of Morgan Stanley, who chairs the firm's Global Wealth Management Asset Allocation and Investment Policy Committee, explains the role of asset allocation in maximizing investment returns to meet life objectives. Brimming with the wisdom gained from years of practical experience, this book is a vital road map to a secure financial future.

The Little Book of Bull Moves in Bear Markets, in which Peter D. Schiff, President of Euro Pacific Capital, Inc., looks at historical downturns in the financial markets to analyze what investment strategies succeeded and shows how to implement various bull moves so that readers can preserve, and even enhance, their wealth within a prosperous or an ailing economy.

The Little Book of Main Street Money, in which Jonathan Clements, award-winning columnist for the *Wall Street Journal* and a director of the new personal finance service myFi, offers 21 commonsense truths about investing to help readers take control of their financial futures.

The Little Book of Safe Money, in which Jason Zweig, best-selling author and columnist for the *Wall Street Journal*, shows the potential pitfalls all investors face and reveals not only how to survive but how to prosper in a volatile and unpredictable economy.

The Little Book of Behavioral Investing, in which James Montier, top-rated strategist, best-selling author and widely regarded leading authority on behavioral finance, identifies the most commonly encountered psychological barriers investors face and offers time-tested ways to avoid and eliminate these behavioral traits so they can go on to make superior returns, and fewer losses.

Upcoming:
The Little Book of Bulletproof Investing by Ben Stein and Phil DeMuth

THE LITTLE BOOK
BIG DIVIDENDS

A Safe Formula for

Guaranteed Returns

CHARLES B. CARLSON

WILEY

John Wiley & Sons, Inc.

Published by John Wiley & Sons, Inc., Hoboken, New Jersey.
Published simultaneously in Canada.

No part of this publication may be reproduced, stored in a retrieval system, or transmitted in any form
or by any means, electronic, mechanical, photocopying, recording, scanning, or otherwise, except as
permitted under Section 107 or 108 of the 1976 United States Copyright Act, without either the prior
written permission of the Publisher, or authorization through payment of the appropriate per-copy fee
to the Copyright Clearance Center, Inc., 222 Rosewood Drive, Danvers, MA 01923, (978) 750-8400,
fax (978) 646-8600, or on the web at www.copyright.com. Requests to the Publisher for permission
should be addressed to the Permissions Department, John Wiley & Sons, Inc., 111 River Street,
Hoboken, NJ 07030, (201) 748-6011, fax (201) 748-6008, or online at http://www.wiley
.com/go/permissions.

Limit of Liability/Disclaimer of Warranty: While the publisher and author have used their best efforts
in preparing this book, they make no representations or warranties with respect to the accuracy or
completeness of the contents of this book and specifically disclaim any implied warranties of
merchantability or fitness for a particular purpose. No warranty may be created or extended by sales
representatives or written sales materials. The advice and strategies contained herein may not be
suitable for your situation. You should consult with a professional where appropriate. Neither the
publisher nor author shall be liable for any loss of profit or any other commercial damages, including
but not limited to special, incidental, consequential, or other damages.

Quadrix® is a registered trademark of Horizon Publishing Services LLC.

For general information on our other products and services or for technical support, please contact our
Customer Care Department within the United States at (800) 762-2974, outside the United States at
(317) 572-3993 or fax (317) 572-4002.

Wiley also publishes its books in a variety of electronic formats. Some content that appears in print
may not be available in electronic books. For more information about Wiley products, visit our web site
at www.wiley.com.

ISBN 978-0-470-56799-9

Printed in the United States of America
10   9   8   7   6   5   4   3   2   1

To Pooks, B&F, and the Valpo 7

Thanks for the love, the smiles,
and the kisses.

Contents

Foreword

❧

Finally—sensible investing made simple. I have known and interviewed Chuck Carlson for over 20 years. He never changes his tune to fit fashion or fad. He just goes along making money, consistently, as his stocks pay dividends. And since only companies that have profits can afford to consistently pay dividends, these stocks have a record of increasing share price, as well.

Now he has made it even easier. In this book, Chuck starts with his basic principle: You can make big money by investing for the long term in dividend-paying stocks. He has even created a free web site to help you find those stocks. And to top it all off, he shows you how to buy many of these stocks—either a one-time purchase or regular small (or large) monthly investments—at no cost, no commissions, no fees, directly from the company.

You might be wondering where this secret has been hiding all these years. Well, it has been hiding in plain sight. For all the years I have known him, Chuck has been trying to explain that investing doesn't have to be complicated, expensive, mathematical, or time-consuming. Maybe it's just that now we're ready to listen!

We've seen genius fail, and technology lead us astray. We've watched Nobel prizewinning economists lose billions, and astrophysicist investment bankers blow trillions. The markets have survived all this hubris. Now it's time to get back to basics.

The idea of investing for dividends sounds rather quaint—something your grandfather did in the olden days. So it might surprise you that from 1926 to the present, dividends have accounted for 43 percent of the total return of the S&P 500 index!

Dividends fell out of favor until recently, because corporate executives were paid bonuses based on stock performance. Thus, they had an incentive to use the company's excess cash to buy back shares, instead of paying dividends with the money. The share buybacks boosted that all-important measure, earnings per share.

With higher reported earnings, stock prices soared. And so did executive bonuses.

We've lived through the sad results of that strategy. We've learned that even the best and brightest can't beat the market forever. You remember that old saying: If you can't beat 'em, join 'em. In *The Little Book of Big Dividends*, Chuck Carlson shows you how to join the stock market's unprecedented record of long-term growth.

First, you have to understand the importance of dividends to overall total return. It will require an amazing suspension of disbelief—in this era of instant gratification—to accept that fact that a 3 percent annual dividend, reinvested regularly, can grow wealth over time. Yet that's just what the S&P 500 has provided, with dividends reinvested, over our lifetimes.

Then, you'll have to step back from the logical presumption that if 3 percent is good, perhaps 10 percent is better. As Chuck explains, an extraordinary dividend yield is a dangerous temptation, a warning of trouble ahead. Perspective is critical. Those who stretch for yield without quality will soon learn the truth of that old saying: "I'm not as concerned with the return *on* my money as I am about the return *of* my money!"

Finally, for those millions of boomers who will soon be searching for income in retirement, this book provides you with a road map to monthly dividend checks that will smooth your retirement planning process. Unlike annuities that offer fixed monthly payouts, dividends can provide increasing stipends as the company grows. Unlike bank CDs, which offer only a guaranteed principal and yield that could be dented by inflation, dividend-paying stocks also offer the potential of growth to keep up with inflation.

So before you dismiss the idea of investing for dividends as either hopelessly old-fashioned or totally boring, remember the old fable of the tortoise and the hare. The tortoise lived to a ripe old age and is enjoying retirement in Florida. So will you, if you'll dedicate at least a portion of your investments to the principles explained here in *The Little Book of Big Dividends*.

Terry Savage

Terry Savage is the nationally syndicated Chicago Sun-Times *financial columnist, and author of four books on personal finance, the latest of which is* The New Savage Number: How Much Money Do You Really Need to Retire? *(John Wiley & Sons, 2009).*

Introduction

———————— ～ ————————

I'M A RARITY IN THAT I HAVE BEEN WITH THE SAME company my entire working career. My first day on the job at Horizon Publishing was August 16, 1982. (Back then the company moniker was Dow Theory Forecasts, named after the investment newsletter that my firm still publishes today.)

There's nothing noteworthy about August 16, 1982. But August 17, 1982, was special.

On that day—my second day on the job, mind you— the Dow Jones Industrial Average rose nearly 39 points. That may not sound like much. But in 1982, it was *huge*. A nearly 5 percent move, or the equivalent in today's terms of 500 points on the Dow.

On that momentous day, the Dow Jones Industrial Average closed at *831.24*. August 17 is pegged by market historians as the beginning of the raging bull market of the 1980s and 1990s, an 18-year period when the Dow Industrials rose from a little over 800 to nearly 11,500 by the end of 1999.

I mention 1982 because of one big similarity I see between the stock market then and now. In 1982, attractive dividend-paying stocks were bountiful. Indeed, many companies were sharing a portion of their profits with shareholders every three months by sending them hefty dividend checks. How big were the dividend checks? It was not uncommon for stocks in 1982 to pay shareholders dividends that equated to a yield of 6 percent or higher. (Think of a stock's dividend yield as the interest rate you get for owning a stock.) And these were quality companies with the potential for their stock prices to rise sharply. It was like shooting fish in a barrel, although I didn't know enough at the time to realize it.

For example, had I the foresight (and the money) to invest a few dollars in some dividend-paying stocks on my first day on the job, I would probably be boogie boarding in Bora Bora right now. Indeed, $5,000 investments in two quality dividend-paying stocks—Philip Morris and Exxon—on August 16, 1982, would now be worth *more than $1 million*. And that's after the market crash of 2008.

And it wasn't as if you had to be Warren Buffett to come up those two gems. Exxon was a Dow stock in 1982, so it was hardly undiscovered. And Philip Morris produced products all of us knew, and some of us even loved. In hindsight, these stocks were no-brainers for dividend-loving investors.

No-brainers that made you rich.

Are there quality, dividend-paying stocks in today's market that are just waiting to make you rich? The answer is yes. Finding them may not be quite as easy as finding them in 1982, but make no mistake:

There are dividend-paying stocks in today's market that will make you rich.

Now Is a Great Time to Be a Dividend Investor. *Really.*

Like 1982, today is an excellent time to be a dividend investor. That may be hard to believe coming on the heels of 2008 and 2009, two of the worst years ever for dividends. How bad? About one out of every eight stocks in the Standard & Poor's 500 Index reduced or eliminated the dividend in 2008. Approximately 15 percent of the companies in the S&P 500 Index cut or omitted dividends in 2009, the highest level ever.

So why do I think there are tremendous opportunities in dividend-paying stocks? Partly because of the massacre of the last few years. A stock's yield is determined by two things—the dividend and the stock price. If a stock price declines, its yield increases (provided, of course, that the company continues to pay the dividend). When stocks were crushed in 2008 and early 2009, the huge price declines lifted dividend yields to levels that, in many cases, I have not seen since 1982.

High dividend yields are only part of the bullish story. Because stocks fell so much in 2008 and early 2009, prices reached ridiculously low levels. Even with the market's rally beginning in March 2009, it is not uncommon to see stocks trading below prices they fetched a decade ago.

The bottom line is that when you consider their bargain-basement prices and high dividend yields, dividend-paying stocks are as attractive today as they have been in nearly three decades.

A Recipe for Riches

If you want the recipe for getting rich in the stock market, here it is: Find stocks with above-average appreciation potential and safe and growing dividends, and buy them at attractive prices.

This book shows you how to do just that.

———————— ∾ ————————

**Dividend-paying stocks are as attractive today as
they have been in nearly three decades.**

In the pages before you is a blueprint for successful
dividend investing. I walk you through the basics—what
a dividend is (and isn't); why, how, and when companies
pay dividends; and why some companies pay big dividends
while others pay no dividends at all. (That's all in Chapter 1.)

In Chapters 2 and 3, I discuss the importance of size
and safety of dividends when considering dividend-paying
stocks, and I introduce you to a simple formula for finding Big, Safe Dividends (BSDs). This formula takes into
account factors most critical to the safety and growth
potential of a company's dividend. I define and discuss
each of these important factors and show you how they
can be used to rank dividend-paying stocks. As you'll
read, my BSD Formula has an excellent track record of
spotlighting attractive dividend-paying stocks while isolating
those where dividend cuts or omissions are most likely.
This chapter also shows the benefits of combining the
BSD Formula with other investment tools to improve
your odds of finding the best stocks for dividends *and*
price appreciation.

My gripe with a lot of investing books is that they tend to be long on theory but short on specific, actionable advice and recommendations. Chapter 4 "names names," taking the ideas and tools from the first three chapters to create lists of my favorite stocks offering big, safe dividends. And we go global. It has never been easier for any investor to buy shares of foreign companies. International investing has become increasingly popular, and this chapter spotlights those foreign stocks that are the most attractive for dividend-seeking investors.

Finding attractive dividend-paying stocks is only one piece of the puzzle. Buying them is another piece. Fortunately, it has never been easier or cheaper for investors to buy stocks with big, safe dividends. Chapter 5 explores the most cost-effective ways for any investor— even those with limited pocketbooks—to buy these stocks. Brokers represent one way to buy these shares, but you can also buy stock directly from the company—the first share and every share—without a broker. With these plans, you can buy shares with very little money down ($250 or less) and pay little or no commission. And it's not just U.S. stocks. A growing number of international stocks, including those with big, safe, dividends, allow any U.S. investor to buy shares directly, without a broker. I'll show you what companies offer the plans and how to get started buying stocks directly.

Inflation is the enemy of any investment program. One way to help stave off the effects of inflation is to make sure your portfolio includes companies with a habit of boosting their dividends. Chapter 6 discusses the importance of dividend growth and highlights stocks with big, safe, and fast-growing dividends.

Americans are getting older. With age comes an increased demand for cash flow. One reason dividend-paying stocks represent an excellent source for cash flow is the ability to synchronize dividend payments with cash-flow needs. Chapter 7 shows you how to organize stocks based on dividend-payment dates in order to construct portfolios that pay you big, safe dividends *every month of the year*—a helpful budgeting tool to meet your monthly bills. If you can sync an iPod, you can sync your investments with your cash needs.

While this book concentrates on dividend-paying common stocks, investors have a growing menu of investment choices to generate cash flow. Preferred stocks, real estate investment trusts (REITs), master limited partnerships, open-end and closed-end mutual funds, and exchange-traded funds (ETFs) are just some of the many investment vehicles investors are turning to for dividends. Chapter 8 takes a walk on the wild side by explaining the pros and cons of these often-risky but potentially high-return investments.

"Buy low and sell high" is every investor's mantra. The reality is, however, that few investors buy low and sell high. We usually buy high and hope to sell higher. The reason is that buying low is hard. Stocks fall because of bad news—a bear market, lousy earnings, product missteps. And avoiding bad news is hotwired into most of our DNA. In order to take advantage of market declines to buy low, you need a strategy that takes emotions out of the decision-making process, a strategy that forces you to buy stocks even when you're afraid. Such an investing strategy exists: dividend reinvestment. With dividend reinvestment, your investing is on autopilot. You buy stock even when you are freaked out by the market. (Actually, when most investors are freaked out by the market is precisely the time you want to be buying.) Dividend reinvestment plans aren't just great tools for forced buying. The plans offer a way to turn a little money into a lot over time. With dividend reinvestment plans, if you don't have enough money to buy a full share of stock, your money will buy a fractional share, and that fractional share is entitled to a fractional part of the dividend. It's like buying stock on the installment plan. And believe it or not, there are some dividend-reinvestment programs that allow you to buy stock with your dividends at a discount to the market price. Chapter 9 discusses these programs.

The book closes with what I call the ultimate big, safe, dividend portfolio. This portfolio features attractive U.S.

and international stocks and funds with big, safe dividends. I show you how to construct the portfolio based on dividend-payment dates (so you'll get a dividend check every month of the year) and how to use low-cost direct-purchase plans to purchase many of the investments. As you'll see, *anyone* can start to build this portfolio with minimal amounts of money.

One reason I wanted to write this book was to dispel a lot of myths about dividend investing. Indeed, much of what is written about dividends is inaccurate or incomplete. Don't get me wrong. Dividends are great, but they are not the free lunch they are so often made out to be in the press. To address some of these myths, as well as to reinforce what I think are important concepts when it comes to dividend investing, you'll find a "Yield!" box at the end of every chapter. What I want you to do when you see Yield! is exactly what you do when you see a Yield sign while driving—slow down and assess the situation before advancing. If you remember only these simple ideas, you'll be way ahead of the pack when it comes to dividend investing.

I have a confession to make. When putting this book together, I was a bit frustrated by its size. In my books, I love to provide lots of lists and tables and statistics and ratings covering hundreds of stocks, but it is tough to do that in such a compact format. I think we did a good job of including the most critical lists and tables throughout the book and especially in the Appendixes at the back of the book. But there was so much more that I wanted to include. The good news is the Internet has virtually unlimited space with which to work, which makes it the perfect complement to my book. To that end, I have provided tons of dividend information on the following web site: www .bigsafedividends.com. You'll find up-to-date dividend ratings, yield information, dividend-payment schedules, and other relevant data on every dividend-paying stock in the Standard & Poor's 1500 Index. The site provides literally a one-stop shop for all things dividends and is a powerful tool for researching dividend-paying stocks. And by the way, all the information is provided *free of charge*.

Time to Get Busy

Finding dividend-paying stocks that will make you rich may not be as easy as shooting fish in a barrel. It isn't August 1982, and the Dow Jones Industrial Average isn't at 831 (thank goodness!), but the big opportunities are out there. By purchasing this book, you have upped your chances dramatically of finding them.

Happy hunting.

Chapter One

The Check Is
in the Mail

—— ❧ ——

Get Paid to Invest with Dividends

THE CONTROLLER OF MY COMPANY IS NAMED PAM. Besides being a great controller, Pam has a great smile, one of those toothy ones that lights up a room. I always enjoy seeing Pam's smiling face, especially every other Friday. Everyone in my company loves to see Pam's smiling face every other Friday. That's when Pam hands us our paychecks.

Payday never gets old. I don't care if you've worked a week or a lifetime. Payday is always a great day, a day never to be taken for granted.

Why is payday great? Besides the obvious, payday represents that weekly, biweekly, or monthly validation that what we do matters, that we aren't simply wasting our time, that we are adding value.

Of course, you may feel other emotions on payday— perhaps jealousy, maybe a little resentment. Still, getting paid is really why we do *anything*. The pay may not always be in dollars. The currency may be that buzz you get when you volunteer your time, coach your daughter's softball team, hike your favorite trail, or send that check to your favorite charity.

Getting paid is why we get up every morning.

And getting paid is why we invest.

Investing may not always feel this way. I didn't exactly feel as if I was getting paid to invest in 2008. It felt as though I was doing the paying. Still, we invest to get paid. Otherwise, we wouldn't do it.

How do we get paid for investing? Two ways:

1. The value of our investment goes up. You buy a stock at $10, and it jumps to $20. You made $10 on your investment. That $10 profit is called a capital gain. If you sell and lock up the profit, you have

a realized capital gain. If you still hold on to the stock, you have an unrealized gain.

2. We receive a portion of the company profits on a regular basis. As a shareholder of a company, you're an owner. As an owner, you have a claim on the profits of the company in proportion to your ownership. The board of directors of your company may choose to keep those profits and reinvest them back in the company. On the other hand, the board may decide to distribute part or all of the profits to the owners. Let's say a company's board has made the decision to disburse 30 percent of its profits that year to shareholders. If profits are $2 million, shareholders receive $600,000. Your claim on that $600,000 depends on your percentage ownership. If you own 1 percent of the company, you'll receive $6,000. That $6,000 is commonly called a "dividend."

Dividends are usually paid quarterly (every three months), although some companies (especially foreign firms) pay dividends only once or twice per year. Companies may differ in the months when they pay their dividends. Some companies pay dividends in March, June, September, and December; some pay in February, May, August, and November; others pay in January, April, July, and October.

Knowing the dividend-payment dates can be useful when constructing a dividend portfolio to provide regular cash flows to meet financial obligations. I'll show you how to construct "dividends-every-month" portfolios in Chapter 7.

A stock's *total return*—the total amount you get paid for investing—is capital gains plus dividends. Let's say you own a stock that goes from $10 per share to $11 per share in a year. During the year, the stock paid $0.50 per share in dividends. The stock's total return for the year is 15 percent ($1 per share in price appreciation plus $0.50 per share in dividend divided by the starting value of $10 per share).

As you can see, dividends represent an important component of a stock's total-return potential. In fact, roughly 40 percent of the stock market's long-run total return comes from dividends.

----------------------------------- ∼ -----------------------------------

**Roughly 40 percent of the stock market's
long-run total return comes from dividends.**

Why Dividends Matter

When you examine the two ways of getting paid to invest—capital gains and dividends—it's natural that dividends have special appeal. A stock's capital-gains potential is influenced significantly by what the market does in a given year. Sure, stocks can buck a downward market. But most don't.

On the other hand, dividends are usually paid whether the broad market is up or down.

The dependability of dividends is a big reason why investors should consider dividends when buying stock. I'm not suggesting that every stock you own must pay a dividend. However, there's something to be said for the bird-in-hand theory of investing—that a steady, dependable dividend stream provides nice ballast to a portfolio's return. Procter & Gamble, the consumer-products giant, has paid a dividend every year since 1891. Procter & Gamble's stock price has not risen every year since 1891. But shareholders who owned the stock at least got paid a little during those down years. They weren't totally dependent on capital gains to get paid.

Another attraction of dividends is that they can grow. Johnson & Johnson, the health-care company, has raised its dividend every year for more than 45 years. Shareholders received those growing dividends regardless of what happened to the stock price in a given year. And the rising dividend stream not only hedged against inflation but also accelerated the payback on investment.

Here's an example of what I mean by payback on investment. If you had invested $5,000 in Johnson & Johnson at the beginning of 1985, held the stock until today, and reinvested dividends along the way, your annual dividends from J&J stock would now be more than $7,100. In other words, your payback on your initial investment via dividends is more 100 percent *every year*.

Now *that's* the power of dividends in an investment program.

To Pay Dividends or Not To Pay Dividends

The stock market is really a market of a bunch of small companies. Probably 80 percent or more of all publicly traded stocks have market capitalizations—market capitalization is figured by multiplying outstanding shares by the per-share stock price—of less than $1 billion. In fact, a healthy chunk of all publicly traded companies have market caps that are less than $100 million. Fewer than 300 companies have market caps above $10 billion.

In short, the typical stock is not IBM or Microsoft or Exxon Mobil. The typical stock is one that you probably never heard of, one in which the firm is quite small and in its primary growth mode.

When you understand that the stock market is really a market of very small companies, you understand why the majority of publicly traded companies don't pay a dividend. A dividend represents an outflow of assets to shareholders. Once dividends are paid, the money is gone, and the firm can no longer use that money to fund growth. Small and growing firms often choose to retain profits in order to have the cash to fund their growth.

Another reason why smaller companies may not pay a dividend is because of the variability of their profits. Small companies may be dependent on a few customers. If orders dry up from one customer, so too do revenues and profits. Implementing a dividend initiates an implicit contract with shareholders, a contract that says that you can depend on this dividend through thick and thin. True, this contract has been a bit frayed by the dividend cuts and omissions seen since late 2007. Historically, however, companies have been extremely reluctant to cut or omit a dividend. Therefore, if a firm is not confident in the stability and dependability of its profit stream, it is unlikely to initiate a dividend.

So what firms pay dividends? They are generally larger, more established companies. Dividend-paying companies have probably experienced their biggest growth spurt and don't require all of their cash flows to fund their operations. Such companies are reasonably confident that their future profitability will support a dividend payment.

Of course, there are exceptions to every rule, and plenty of smaller companies pay dividends. Still, out of the some 4,000 firms my firm tracks via our Quadrix stock-rating system (I'll tell you about Quadrix later in the book), less than 38 percent pay dividends. And those dividend payers tend to have market capitalizations, on average, of $8.4 billion versus the average market cap of non–dividend-paying stocks of $1.5 billion.

No Profits, No Dividends

A stock's dividend represents the cash flows companies pay their common shareholders. These cash flows are ultimately paid out of profits or, technically, "retained earnings" of the company. That's pretty basic stuff, right? It's obvious that if a company doesn't generate profits, it probably isn't generating the cash flow that can be used to pay dividends. Yet you'd be surprised how many investors tend to ignore the relationship between profits and dividends when choosing dividend-paying stocks.

***

Dividends are ultimately paid out of a company's profits, so pay attention to the relationship between the two.

***

You may have owned companies that had a bad year but still paid their dividend, but that's not a game that can be played indefinitely. Companies can borrow money to pay their dividend. They can dip into cash reserves to pay their dividend. But at some point, a firm that isn't earning its dividend will not pay the dividend.

A useful tool for examining the relationship between profits and dividends is a stock's payout ratio. The payout ratio reflects the percentage of a company's earnings that are paid out in the form of dividends. A firm that has profits of $2 per share and pays $1 per share in dividends has a payout ratio of 0.5 (1 divided by 2).

The higher the payout ratio, the more danger the company is in of reducing or eliminating the dividend if problems develop. The payout ratio is the single most powerful factor in analyzing the health, stability, and growth potential of a stock's dividend. For that reason, the payout ratio carries the highest weighting in my Big, Safe Dividend (BSD) Formula discussed in Chapter 3.

What's My Yield?

Many investors like to compare dividends on stocks to the interest paid on bank CDs or money market accounts or the coupon payments paid on bonds. Although this is a bit of an apples-to-oranges comparison (the risks of stocks are decidedly greater than the risks of bank CDs or most bonds), the comparison is useful for understanding the concept of *yield*. The yield on your money market account is the same as the interest rate; that is, if you put $1,000 in a money market account that promises to pay you $20 in interest over the next year, the interest rate (or yield) is 2 percent ($20 divided by $1,000).

A stock's dividend yield is computed the same way. You take the amount of dividends paid over the last year and divide by the stock price. For example, a stock that trades at $10 per share and paid $0.50 per share in dividends over the last 12 months has a yield of 5 percent ($0.50 divided by 10).

Most investors use a stock's indicated dividend to compute yield. The indicated dividend is computed by taking the stock's most recent dividend payment and annualizing it. Thus, for a stock that paid $0.25 per share in its most recent quarter, the indicated annual dividend would be $1 per share ($0.25 multiplied by four quarters if the company pays quarterly dividends). And if the stock currently trades for $20, the indicated yield is 5 percent ($1 divided by $20).

While important, yield should not be the primary determinant for stock selection. Investors too often ignore the fact that yield is a pretty good proxy for risk. An unusually high yield can foreshadow big problems at a company. In fact, a high yield is an excellent predictor of dividend cuts or omissions. I'll discuss more about the relationship of yield and risk in Chapter 2.

No Free Lunch

While dividends are often referred to as an investor "free lunch," that's not exactly true. A dividend is not free money for shareholders. A company cannot pay out dividends to shareholders without affecting its market value.

Think of your own finances. If you constantly paid out cash to family members, your net worth would decrease. It's no different for a company. Money that a company pays out to shareholders is money that is no longer part of the asset base of the corporation. It's money that can no longer be used to reinvest and grow the company. That reduction in the company's "wealth" has to be reflected in a downward adjustment in the stock price.

You may be surprised to learn that a stock price adjusts downward when a dividend is paid. The adjustment may not be easily observed amidst the daily price fluctuations of a typical stock. But the adjustment does happen.

This adjustment is much more obvious when a company pays a "special dividend." A good example is Microsoft's special $3-per-share dividend it paid to shareholders in 2004. Following the payment, the downward adjustment in Microsoft stock was readily apparent.

Dating My Ex

This downward adjustment in the stock price takes place on the ex-dividend date. Typically, the ex-dividend date is two business days prior to the record date. The key thing about the ex-dividend date is that it represents the cut-off point for receiving the dividend. You have to own a stock prior to the ex-dividend date in order to receive the next dividend payment. If you buy a stock on or after the ex-dividend date, you are not entitled to the next paid dividend.

While this may sound unfair, remember that the stock price adjusts downward to reflect the dividend payment. Therefore, while you are not entitled to the dividend if you buy on or after the ex-dividend date, you are paying a lower price for the shares.

An example best shows the interworking of the ex-dividend date, record date, and payable date:

Declaration Date	Ex-Dividend Date	Record Date	Payable Date
11/10/09	11/27/09	12/1/09	12/30/09

On November 10, 2009, XYZ, Inc. declares a dividend payable on December 30, 2009, to its shareholders. XYZ also announces that shareholders of record on the company's books on or before December 1, 2009 are entitled to the dividend. The stock would then go ex-dividend two business days before the record date. In this example, the record date falls on a Tuesday. Excluding weekends and holidays, the ex-dividend is two business days before the record date—in this case on the preceding Friday, November 27. Anyone who bought the stock on Friday or after would not get the dividend (that dividend goes to the seller of the shares). Those who purchase before the ex-dividend date receive the dividend.

I wish I had a dime every time an investor told me that he had been ripped off by a company because he didn't receive a dividend that he thought he was owed. Much of the confusion stems from the record date. Many investors believe that if they buy on the record date, they are entitled to the dividend. However, stock trades do not "settle" on the day you buy them. You need to be a shareholder on the record date, which means you have to buy *before* the record date. The ex-dividend date essentially reflects the settlement period.

I know this may sound a bit confusing, but the key date to know is the ex-dividend date. That is the date in which the stock price adjusts to reflect the next dividend payment. And if you want that dividend payment, you have to buy the stock prior to the ex-dividend date.

Capture the Dividend—Not!

At this point you may be thinking to yourself: If all I want is the dividend, why can't I just buy the stock just prior to the ex-dividend date and sell on the ex-dividend date? In that way, I can capture the dividend payment—free money.

Not quite. Remember that the stock price adjusts for the dividend payment. Say you buy 200 shares of stock at $24 per share on November 26, one day before the ex-dividend date of November 27. And you sell the stock at the close of November 27. And the stock pays a quarterly dividend of $0.50 per share. The stock price will adjust downward on November 27 to reflect the $0.50 payment.

It's possible that, despite this adjustment, the stock could actually close on November 27 at a higher level. It's also possible that the stock price could close November 27 at a level lower than the $23.50 price suggested by the $0.50 adjustment to reflect the $0.50 dividend.

Let's assume for the sake of this example, the stock adjusts perfectly, and you sell at $23.50 per share. Are you better or worse off for capturing the dividend? Well, you'll receive $0.50 per share in the dividend. But you'll lose $0.50 per share because of the decline in the stock price. So it would appear to be a wash. But what about taxes? Aren't dividends currently taxed at a maximum 15 percent rate? I'll get into dividends and taxes a little later in this chapter, but for now the answer is "yes," but with a catch. In order to receive the preferred 15 percent tax rate on dividends, you must hold the stock for a minimum number of days. That minimum period is 61 days within the 121-day period surrounding the ex-dividend date. The 121-day period begins 60 days before the ex-dividend date. When counting the number of days, the day that the stock is disposed is counted, but not the day the stock is acquired.

If the stock is not held at least 61 days in the 121-day period surrounding the ex-dividend date, the dividend does not receive the favorable 15 percent rate and is taxed at your ordinary tax rate.

To recap your dividend capture strategy:

1. You paid $4,800 (plus commission) to purchase 200 shares of stock.
2. Because you bought before the ex-dividend date, you're entitled to the dividend of $0.50 per share, or $100. But because you didn't hold the stock for 61 days, you'll pay taxes at your ordinary tax rate. Let's assume you are in the 28 percent tax bracket. That means your take after taxes is $72.
3. You sold 200 shares at $23.50 for $4,700, a loss of $100 (plus commissions). You now have a "realized" short-term loss, which you can offset against realized capital gains or, if you have no realized gains, up to $3,000 of ordinary income.

Was your dividend-capture strategy in this instance a winner? Not really. You're out the commissions to buy and sell the shares. You have a realized loss that you may or may not be able to write off immediately (depending on the amount of realized gains and losses you already have). And you lose the preferred 15 percent tax rate on your dividends because you didn't hold the stock long enough.

I'm sure you could construct a hypothetical in which capturing the dividend provides a big windfall. But the key point is that there are no free lunches. Dividend-capture strategies don't have all upside and no downside. Between commissions, taxes, and downward adjustments for dividend payments, it's not easy to profit from dividend-capture strategies.

Dividends and Taxes

Qualified dividends are currently taxed at a maximum rate of 15 percent. The rate drops to 0 percent for lower-income individuals in the 10 percent to 15 percent tax brackets for ordinary income.

What constitutes a "qualified" dividend? Most dividends paid by domestic companies are qualified. And many dividends paid by foreign companies also qualify for the preferred tax rate. However, distributions paid by real estate investment trusts, master limited partnerships, and other similar "pass-through" entities may not qualify for favored tax status.

Also, as demonstrated in our dividend-capture example, dividends that are paid on shares that are not held at least

61 days in the 121-day period surrounding the ex-dividend date are not "qualified" dividends.

How dividends are taxed is very important when considering investments for cash flow. Interest on money markets and bank CDs is taxed at ordinary tax rates. So are interest payments on bonds. That means a person in the top tax bracket pays taxes on interest payments up to 35 percent. Compare that to the maximum 15 percent tax on dividends, and the "after-tax" returns are significantly better with dividends.

Say you put $100,000 into a bank CD paying 2 percent annual interest. You'll receive $2,000 in interest. If you are in the top tax bracket, your after-tax yield (assuming the investment is held outside of a retirement account) is 1.3 percent. (You arrive at that percentage by applying your tax rate of 35 percent to the $2,000 interest payment, leaving you with after-tax interest of $1,300, for an after-tax yield of 1.3 percent). If you invest the same $100,000 in a basket of stocks paying 2 percent annually in dividends, you'll receive $2,000 in dividends but only lose $300 to taxes (15 percent of $2,000), for an after-tax yield of 1.7 percent ($1,700 in after-tax dividends divided by $100,000 investment).

When comparing investments for cash flow, smart investors look at both pre-tax and after-tax yields. After all, it's not what you make. It's what you keep.

The bad news is that the preferred tax rate on dividends is in jeopardy. Unless an extension is granted or new rules enacted, the current tax rates on dividends expire at the end of 2010.

Obviously, the tax rate on dividends has huge implications for dividend-hungry investors. Will higher tax rates, if enacted, reduce the appeal of dividend-paying stocks? Will investors dump their dividend-paying stocks once the favored tax rate has expired? Perhaps, although tax rates on dividends cannot be viewed in a vacuum. What happens to the tax rates on capital gains (the current 15 percent maximum tax rate on realized long-term capital gains also expires at the end of 2010) will have a bearing on the relative attractiveness of dividend-paying stocks. And the type of stock-market environment we have after 2010 will impact interest in dividend-paying stocks. Finally, the graying of America will continue to drive a need for cash flow, which should be a plus for dividend-paying stocks.

In short, don't count out dividend-paying stocks because taxes on dividends may go higher. Plenty of reasons will still exist for investors to seek dividend-paying stocks.

Yield!

- *Dividends matter.* Nearly half of the stock market's long-term total return comes from dividends.

- *Less taxing.* When comparing yields on investments, remember to take into account the favorable tax rates (maximum 15 percent) on qualified dividends. After-tax yields are what really matter.

- *No free money.* Stock prices adjust downward for dividend payments. Don't let anyone tell you differently.

- *Bye-bye dividend.* A company that isn't making a profit is a company that isn't going to be paying a dividend for long.

- *Buy before the ex.* Want the dividend? Buy the stock before the ex-dividend date.

Chapter Two

Super Size Me, without the Heartburn

Size Matters When It Comes to Dividends, but So Does Safety

IS BIGGER BETTER? Depends.

Bigger is better when it comes to buffets and bank accounts, but not bellies and ballerinas.

And bigger is not always better when it comes to dividends and yields.

In 2007 Thornburg Mortgage, a real estate investment trust (REIT), was a favorite stock of income investors. The big appeal? A dividend yield that—at one point during the year—exceeded 20 percent. How could you go wrong getting 20 percent plus on your money? Even if the stock went down a little, you would still be well ahead of the game, right?

Thornburg Mortgage no longer offers a 20 percent dividend yield. The company went bankrupt in 2009, a victim of the credit crunch that annihilated many high-yielding real estate investment trusts. Investors who bought Thornburg Mortgage because of that big dividend and big yield lost their entire investment.

The ironic thing is that the yield of 20 percent plus on Thornburg was basically telling investors that a dividend omission—and possibly something much worse—was about to befall the company. Many investors chose to ignore this signal, instead focusing solely on the big dividend.

The big dividend that turned out to be illusory.

Now compare Thornburg Mortgage to FPL Group, the holding company for Florida Power & Light. In 2007, FPL Group was yielding around 3 percent. Is that a big yield? I'm sure investors who bought Thornburg Mortgage didn't think so. They were wrong.

- In 2007, the yield on the S&P 500 Index was less than 2 percent. FPL Group's yield was 50 percent higher at nearly 3 percent.
- The yield on short-term Treasuries was less than 3 percent toward the end of 2007. And individuals paid taxes on interest on T-bills at their ordinary tax rates, not the maximum 15 percent tax rate on qualified dividends. Thus, FPL's after-tax yield compared favorably to after-tax yields on cash instruments.
- While Thornburg was omitting its dividend and going bankrupt, FPL Group was increasing its dividend—nearly 9 percent in 2008 and 6 percent in 2009.
- Thornburg Mortgage is dead today. FPL is very much alive and well, yielding more than 3 percent and posting decent capital gains for investors.

So who had the "bigger" dividend and yield—Thornburg Mortgage or FPL Group?

Yield Equals Risk, More or Less

It's a cliché, but it tends to be true when it comes to dividend investing: if it seems too good to be true, it usually is. Thornburg's yield of more than 20 percent, at a time

[24] THE LITTLE BOOK OF BIG DIVIDENDS

when the S&P 500 Index was yielding 2 percent, should have seemed too good to be true. And I think in their heart of hearts, most investors—even those who bought the stock—knew the yield was too good to be true. But they bought anyway. Why? Greed. Need. Hope. All big drivers of investment mistakes.

If you take only one thing away from this book, let it be the following: *Dividend yield is a pretty good proxy for investment risk.*

If a stock's yield is considerably higher than the yield of the typical stock in its sector—perhaps three percentage points or more higher—that's a red flag that something may be amiss. (You can see what the average yield is for any sector in *Value Line Investment Survey*, which is available at most libraries.) If a stock's yield is significantly higher than the overall market as measured by the Dow Jones Industrial Average or S&P 500 index—perhaps four or five times the market yield—that's a red flag. (You can find dividend yields for the Dow Industrials and S&P 500 Index every week in the Market Laboratory pages of *Barron's*.) If a stock's yield is considerably higher than its long-run average yield—perhaps twice or three times its historical yield—that's a red flag. (*Value Line* is a good source for a stock's historical dividend yield.)

Why is dividend yield a good proxy for risk? Remember that yield requires two data points—dividend and stock price.

A stock's yield rises if two things happen: (1) the dividend increases and/or (2) the stock price falls. Usually, extraordinarily high dividend yields don't result from increasing dividends. They result from plummeting stock prices.

Even smart investors will run into trouble when it comes to discerning whether a company's dividend is in trouble.

I've been a professional investor for 27 years. I have a Chartered Financial Analyst (CFA) designation. I have undergraduate and graduate degrees from two of the finest universities in the country (Northwestern University and University of Chicago). I've written nine books on investing. I've appeared as an "expert" countless times on financial radio and television programs. And I'm telling you that *I* am not smarter than the market when it comes to evaluating the safety of dividends. *No one* is smarter than the market when it comes to spotlighting dividends at risk.

The stock market is not perfectly efficient, but one area where the market really shines is in telling investors when a dividend is in trouble. The market sends that signal by hammering a stock. As the stock crumbles, the dividend yield rises. (Stock prices react more quickly to investment risk than boards of directors, which is why the stock price will decline in a big way before the dividend is cut or omitted.) Investors who choose to ignore a stock's price action when evaluating the safety of the dividend make a huge mistake. Investors made that mistake with Thornburg Mortgage and other high-yielding REITs. Investors made that mistake with many high-yielding banks and financial-services firms in 2008. And investors chasing high yields will continue to make that mistake in the future.

Don't be one of those investors.

Dividend yield is a pretty good proxy for investment risk.

Finding Big, *Safe* Dividends

Just because yield is a proxy for risk doesn't mean investors can't find companies offering big, *safe* dividends and yields. In fact, I see more quality companies paying big, safe dividends now than I've seen in decades. You just need to evaluate dividends and yields differently. Smart investors consider the following:

- *Safety and dependability of the dividend.* As Thornburg Mortgage showed, it doesn't matter if a stock yields 20 percent. If the dividend is omitted and the stock price goes to zero, that big dividend was really no dividend at all. First and foremost, a "big" dividend is one that is going to be around today, tomorrow, and well into the future.

- *Capital-gains potential of the stock.* Remember that yield is only one part of a stock's total return. You can't ignore a stock's capital-gains prospects when evaluating the size of the dividend and yield. So what if a company pays a "big" yield of 8 percent if the investment loses 50 percent of its value?

- *Yields on alternative investments.* When I first started in this business in the early 1980s, it was not uncommon to see stocks yielding 6 percent or higher. Of course, at that time inflation was sky high (in 1981, the annualized average inflation rate was 10 percent), and yields on cash and fixed-income investments were in the teens. Were those 6 percent yields "big" yields? I suppose in absolute terms they were, but they weren't exactly big yields when compared to other investments. When you're evaluating the attractiveness of a stock's yield, ask yourself, *How does the yield compare to alternatives?* If the yield compares favorably, even if the absolute yield may be a bit underwhelming, then it may be bigger than you think.

- *Yields on comparable investments.* If you are considering a stock that yields 4 percent when the S&P 500 Index is yielding 2 percent, it's fair to label that stock's yield as "big." After all, it's twice the market yield. And if the yield of a particular utility stock is 5 percent when the average yield for utilities is 4 percent, it's reasonable to call that a "big" yield. Of course, if the yield on the utility is 15 percent when the typical utility is yielding 4 percent, that's not a big yield. It's a yield about to disappear. You should start to get nervous if you see a stock yield three percentage points or more above the average yield for its sector. Again, you can get a nice feel for sector yields in *Value Line Investment Survey*.

- *Pre-tax versus after-tax yields*. A stock that yields 2 percent actually has a higher yield than a bank CD that yields the same 2 percent. Why? Because you'll pay a lower tax rate on dividend income versus interest on the bank CD. Thus, your after-tax yield is greater on the stock than on the bank CD. When considering investments for cash flow, remember to look at both pre-tax and after-tax yields if the investment is held outside of a retirement account.

- *Dividend-growth potential*. Which would you rather have—a stock that pays a yield of 7 percent with no chance of dividend growth, or a stock that yields 4.5 percent with excellent dividend-growth prospects? Actually, that it is one of those unanswerable

questions. Ultimately you want the stock that generates the best total returns over time. And you don't
know how each of these stocks will perform in terms
of their price appreciation. Still, just looking at
the dividend yields and long-term cash flows for a
moment, let's return to the question—which one
would you rather have? Most income-oriented investors would take the 7 percent yielder since the
current cash flow is better than what you get with
the 4.5 percent yielder. That may be true this year,
but what about 5 years from now, or 10 years, or
20 years? Assuming the 4.5 percent yielder's stock
price never changes, the dividend would have to
increase 55 percent for the stock to yield 7 percent. If
a company increases its dividend 9 percent per year,
the dividend would jump 55 percent in roughly five
years. And if the dividend continues to increase at
9 percent per year, the dividend would double in
another eight years, and double again in another
eight years. My point is that the impulse of most
dividend investors is to focus on current income.
But if you hold stocks for the long term, you need
to factor dividend-growth potential into the equation
when judging the size of a stock's dividend yield.
(You can use the "rule of 72" to run what-if scenar-
ios on dividend growth. The rule of 72 says that

you can determine how quickly money will double by dividing the yield or interest rate into 72. For example, a dividend will double in approximately 10 years if it grows on average 7.2 percent per year. If the dividend grows an average of 10 percent per year, it doubles in 7.2 years.)

The last point I want to make is that using your own personal needs to determine whether a dividend is "big" or not is irrelevant and dangerous. Dividend investors make this mistake all of the time. The thinking goes something like this—"I *need* a yield of at least 6 percent on my investments in order to pay my bills and fund my lifestyle. I *need* a yield that big and will only buy stocks yielding 6 percent."

Big mistake.

Just because you *need* a 6 percent yield doesn't imply any special investment merit to stocks with that yield. The market doesn't know or care that you need 6 percent. Those stocks don't know or care that you need 6 percent. You can't pick stocks based purely on your own personal income needs. It's done all of the time, and it's a deadly mistake. *You have to pick dividend-paying stocks on their merits, not your needs.*

Because investors too often base stock selection on needs, they start the investment-selection process by filtering stocks based on yield. That approach tends to limit the investment pool to stocks that ultimately have high yields, many of which may have high yields for ominous reasons—lousy profit potential, a stock price that has been hammered, little hope for dividend growth, a looming dividend cut, and so on. That's the opportunity set that yield-only investors create, and it's not pretty.

Pick dividend-paying stocks on their *merits*, not your *needs*.

A better approach is to filter stocks based on total-return merits and then use yield as a second filter. I talk more about this approach—along with unveiling my formula for finding big, safe dividends—in the next chapter.

Yield!

- *Yield not to temptation.* Yield and risk are joined at the hip. Stocks with yields that seem too good to be true are disasters waiting to happen. Avoid them.

- *Too much of a "good" thing can kill you.* If a stock yields more than 3 percentage points above its peers and more than five times the S&P 500 yield, just say no.

- *Avoid pond scum.* Relegating your investment "fishing pond" to only the highest-yielding stocks is a recipe for disaster. Just ask anyone who did this in 2008.

Chapter Three

If Einstein Was a Dividend Investor

The Little Formula That Finds the Biggest, Safest Dividends

$$E = mc^2$$

What I appreciate most about Einstein's Theory of Relativity is its *conciseness*. While a huge amount of science, physics, and math are behind this seemingly simple formula; Einstein's brilliance was distilling all of that mind-bending stuff into an equation consisting of just three factors—energy, mass, and speed of light.

Less is usually more when it comes to formulas, including those for investing. The fewer moving parts in an investing methodology, the easier it is to implement and monitor.

I spent much of the last chapter showing that finding big, safe, dividend-paying stocks is not as easy as simply buying the highest-yielding stocks. That approach is *too* simple. The travails of dividend stocks since 2007 bear this out. For the 12 months that ended on September 30, 2009, there were 926 negative dividend actions taken by corporations, according to Standard & Poor's. That's out of the approximately 7,000 publicly traded companies that report dividend information to S&P.

Still, there is a way to tilt the odds in your favor. And while I'm no Einstein, I believe he would appreciate the simplicity of my methodology.

I call it my Big, Safe, Dividend (BSD) Formula.

Actually, I have two versions of the BSD Formula. The Basic BSD Formula is discussed in this chapter. For those of you who want more science in your stock picking, the Advanced BSD Formula is discussed in Appendix A at the back of the book. If you like the returns of the Basic BSD Formula, you'll absolutely *love* the returns of the Advanced BSD Formula.

Basic BSD Formula for Stock Selection

The basic formula starts with two simple premises:

1. A company cannot pay dividends if it doesn't have the money to pay dividends.
2. You need to choose stocks that have attractive *total-return* potential, not just dividend return.

In addressing those two points, my basic BSD Formula looks at just two data points:

1. Payout ratio
2. Overall Quadrix score

Both are explained in detail below.

Payout Ratio

A stock's payout ratio measures how much of a company's profit is paid out in dividends. The payout ratio addresses the first premise: Can the company maintain and grow the dividend?

For example, a company earning $2 per share in profits and paying out $1 per share in dividends has a payout ratio of 0.5 (1 divided by 2). Obviously, if a company pays out more in dividends than profits, the dividend will not be sustained. If a company pays out a small portion of its profits in the form of dividends, there's cushion for the dividend to grow or at least be maintained, even if profits decline.

The payout ratio is perhaps the most powerful tool for getting a quick snapshot of a company's ability to maintain and grow its dividend.

The nice thing about a payout ratio is that it is easy to compute: Take the stock's annual indicated dividend (compute this by taking the most recent quarterly dividend and multiplying by four) and divide by trailing 12-month per-share earnings. Alternatively, you can create a forward-looking payout ratio by (1) taking the stock's annual indicated dividend and (2) dividing by the consensus full-year earnings estimate of Wall Street analysts who follow the stock. All of these data, including earnings estimates, are available at Yahoo!Finance (finance.yahoo.com).

Let's say the latest quarterly dividend payment for XYZ Company is $0.50 per share. The annual indicated dividend is $2 ($0.50 multiplied by four quarters). The analysts' consensus earnings estimate for the fiscal year is $4 per share. The forward-looking payout ratio would be 0.5 ($2 in per-share dividends divided by $4 in per-share profits).

If you use analysts' earnings estimates, realize that these are what the name implies—estimates. Analysts' estimates are oftentimes wrong. If you want to compute a conservative payout ratio that looks forward, use the low-end analysts' estimate. (The range of analysts' earnings estimates is provided on Yahoo!Finance.)

What constitutes a "safe" payout ratio? I get nervous when I see payout ratios north of 60 percent. Some industries that pay out the bulk of cash flows to shareholders in the form of dividends—such as real estate investment trusts, master limited partnerships, royalty trusts, and so on—will have payout ratios well above 90 percent. If you use the 60 percent threshold (0.6) for payout ratios, you would never own those stocks. And that wouldn't be the worst thing in the world. Indeed, these investments, though typically sporting big dividend yields, can have volatile dividend streams. I'll talk about these exotic dividend investments in Chapter 8.

For now, though, use 60 percent as your upper limit for the payout ratio. Yes, you'll miss some opportunities in stocks with payout ratios exceeding 0.6. But you'll also stay out of trouble.

------------------------------ ∼ ------------------------------

The payout ratio is perhaps the most powerful tool for getting a quick snapshot of whether a company will maintain and grow its dividend.

Overall Quadrix Score

The second issue that needs to be addressed when searching for Big, Safe Dividend stocks is the following: What is the stock's total-return potential?

All too often, investors pick stocks based on a single data point or small set of data points that jibe with their approach. Value investors gravitate toward companies that are most attractive because of their price/earnings ratios or discounted cash flow. Growth disciples focus on companies with the best sales and earnings growth. Momentum investors look for the strongest stock-price action. And dividend investors focus on yield.

The problem with such narrow approaches is that if your entire strategy is based on a single metric or on a small set of correlated metrics, your portfolio could take a major hit by the time you realize that you've bet on the wrong metric and that a change is needed.

My firm's Quadrix stock-rating system is an excellent tool for spotlighting stocks demonstrating balanced and broad strength. Quadrix ranks more than 4,000 stocks based on more than 100 different variables across six categories:

1. Momentum (growth in earnings, cash flow, and sales)
2. Quality (return on investment, return on equity, return on assets)
3. Value (price/sales, price/earnings, price/book ratios)

4. Financial strength (debt levels)
5. Earnings estimates
6. Performance (relative stock price performance)

Within each category, some variables are weighted more heavily, based on past effectiveness. To compute an Overall Score, Quadrix uses a weighted average of the six category scores. The Overall Score is a percentile ranking, so a stock that has an Overall Quadrix Score of 90 means it scores better than 90 percent of the stocks in the Quadrix universe. The best way to use Quadrix is to focus on stocks that score in the upper quartile (75 and above out of a possible 100).

The key thing to understand about Quadrix is that the second piece of the Basic BSD Formula requires some quantitative judgment of the investment merit of the company. Alternatives to Quadrix that are available at libraries or online include *Value Line's* Timeliness and Safety Rankings (focus on either No. 1 or No. 2–rated stocks for Safety and Timeliness), S&P's "Star" Rating System (available to customers of many discount brokers—focus on four- and five-star stocks), or Morningstar's stock-rating system (available at www.morningstar.com—focus on four- and five-star stocks).

I realize that using the Basic or Advanced BSD Formulas may present challenges for investors, especially those who don't have access to Quadrix, *Value Line*, Yahoo!Finance, or other online investment tools. To make your lives easier, my firm has set up a free web site—www.bigsafedividends.com—that provides payout ratios, Overall Quadrix scores, and BSD scores for every dividend-paying stock in the S&P 1500 Index. This information is updated weekly and should provide you with an easy way to see how stocks of interest score.

Beat the Market

Armed with these two data points—a stock's payout ratio and the Overall Quadrix score—what should an investor do next? An approach that has proven to be quite powerful in producing market-beating returns while avoiding dividend cuts is the following:

Filter 1: Focus on stocks with payout ratios of 60 percent (0.6) or lower

Filter 2: Narrow the field to stocks with Overall Quadrix scores of 75 and higher

If you follow this simple approach, you are likely to find stocks with safe and growing dividends that offer above-average total returns.

Of course, the proof is in the proverbial pudding. How would you have done had you used this simple approach to pick dividend-paying stocks?

- Had you created a portfolio at the beginning of each year of all of the stocks in the S&P 1500 Index that met the above criteria (payout ratios of 60 percent or lower and Overall Quadrix scores of 75 and higher), you would have outperformed the S&P 1500 Index on average by *more than four percentage points per year* going back to the end of 1994—a time period that captures both very strong and very weak stock markets.

- Not only were the Basic BSD Formula's returns much better than the S&P 1500 Index, but you achieved those superior returns at a *lower risk level* than the index as measured by standard deviation.

- 2008 was one of the worst years ever for dividends, so it serves as a useful litmus test for the Basic BSD Formula. Of the stocks in the S&P 1500 Index that met our selection criteria (payout ratios of 60 percent or lower and Overall Quadrix scores of 75 and higher) at the beginning of 2008, 60 percent *increased* their dividends during the year. The stocks in our preferred group, while only making up approximately one-quarter of all dividend-paying stocks in the S&P 1500 Index, accounted for 43 percent of all dividend increases in the index during the year.

- Of the 245 stocks in the S&P 1500 Index that met our selection criteria at the beginning of 2008, only 12 cut or omitted their dividends during the year. That's less than 5 percent. To put that percentage in perspective, you had only a 1-in-20 chance of owning a stock that cut its dividend in 2008 if you followed our Basic BSD Formula at the beginning of the year: not perfect, but not bad considering 2008 was a horrible year for dividend cuts and omissions. (The Advanced BSD Formula was even better on this score. Only *two* stocks from the S&P 1500 Index meeting the Advanced BSD Formula selection criteria at the beginning of 2008 cut their dividends during the year.)

You may be thinking that this is back-testing your way into this methodology. Actually, it isn't. We came up with this simple formula based on our own experience, and then went back to see how it worked.

The next logical question is: What about yield? Nowhere did I mention a stock's yield in this equation. Picking stocks based solely on yield is a loser's game. My firm has done lots of research on this, and I can tell you that high-yielding stocks as a group don't outperform the market. What the Basic BSD Formula does is pinpoint good-quality stocks that have a safe dividend that is likely to be increased over time.

If you want to consider yields after you have run stocks through the first two screens (for example, "filter 3—pick stocks with yields greater than 2 percent"), that's fine by me. But don't start focusing on yield before you've done the analysis that tells you that (1) the dividend is safe, (2) the dividend is likely to grow, and (3) the stock is worthy from an overall investment standpoint.

Don't look at yield until you've analyzed the safety of the dividend, the ability for the dividend to grow, and the overall investment merit of the stock.

One criticism of the Basic BSD Formula is that you will never own such high-yielding investments as real estate investment trusts (REITs), master limited partnerships (MLPs), or royalty trusts. These investments all have payout ratios well above 60 percent, thus eliminating them from consideration. I realize that may turn off some investors who love high-yielding stocks. So be it. I felt having a simple formula that anyone can follow trumped the possible exclusion of certain investment vehicles. If you can't live without REITs, MLPs, and royalty trusts, you may find the Advanced BSD Formula more to your liking. The Advanced Formula, while giving ample weighting to pay-out ratio, does not eliminate a stock if its payout ratio is

greater than 60 percent. See Appendix A for more on the
Advanced BSD Formula, including a list of high-scoring
BSD stocks with yields up to 11 percent.

Yield!

- *It pays to use this ratio.* Payout ratio is the single most powerful
  tool for assessing the health of a company's dividend. Ignore it
  at your own peril.

- *Don't pick one without the other.* Buy stocks that score well on
  dividend criteria *and* investment criteria. Remember: the best
  stocks to own are those with the best *total-return* potential.

- *Help is just a click away.* Not into math? Go to www.bigsafe
  dividends.com for current BSD scores and information on
  all dividend-paying stocks in the S&P 1500 Index.

Chapter Four

The World Is Your Oyster

Dividend Pearls from around the Globe

I'VE BEEN TO NEW ZEALAND TWICE since 2007. It's a bear getting there (about 22 hours from Chicago), but the payoff is *spectacular*. The country presses all the right buttons:

- Lots of water (New Zealand is basically two big islands surrounded by the Pacific Ocean to the east and the Tasman Sea to the west).

- Majestic terrain (much of *The Lord of the Rings* trilogy was filmed on New Zealand's South Island).
- Plenty of space (only four million or so people live in New Zealand, with about one-third of the population concentrated in Auckland).

And one special bonus—No Snakes! When you enter New Zealand, the customs inspectors are just as concerned with what's on your shoes (or "trekkers," as they called mine) as what's in your travel bags. New Zealand is very, very, *very* watchful as to what comes into its pristine environment. That's partly the reason there are no snakes and very few creepy-crawly things.

If you get the chance, don't worry that it takes a day to get there . . . or that you'll have to drive on the other side of the road . . . or that the cuisine will remind you that the country was once a British colony. Just go!

My love for New Zealand does not dilute my love for the United States. I've been to all but 4 of the 50 states, and I can say I have found something to like in all of them. (I confess I'm still looking for the silver lining in Oklahoma, but that is probably a result of a car-trip-without-air-conditioning I endured in the Sooner State in the summer of 1985.)

My point is that the United States has lots of cool places to see and experience. And so does New Zealand, or Australia (another very cool place), and virtually every country in the world.

The same goes with dividend investing. There are lots of attractive U.S. dividend stocks. And there are lots of attractive dividend payers based outside the United States. Smart investors include all of them when building a portfolio of big, safe dividends.

The rest of this chapter "names names," giving you some of the best dividend stocks in the United States and around the globe based on our Basic and Advanced BSD Formulas and Quadrix ratings.

Steady Eddies

The following stocks score well in our Basic BSD Formula (payout ratio of 0.6 and below and Overall Quadrix score of at least 75) and represent some of the most consistent dividend payers. Hence the name "Steady Eddies"—stocks that aren't necessarily going to be at the top of the leader board in any given year but offer steady and dependable dividends, above-average dividend growth, and decent capital-gains potential. Each of the stocks yields at least 2.0 percent. Ticker symbols are in parentheses.

Abbott Labs (ABT)

Aflac (AFL)

Automatic Data Processing (ADP)

Campbell Soup (CPB)

Chubb (CB)

Clorox (CLX)

ConAgra Foods (CAG)

General Mills (GIS)

Hasbro (HAS)

Johnson & Johnson (JNJ)

Kellogg (K)

Kimberly-Clark (KMB)

Lockheed Martin (LMT)

McDonald's (MCD)

PepsiCo (PEP)

Procter & Gamble (PG)

Sysco (SYY)

Travelers (TRV)

Not surprisingly, many of these stocks are household names. Johnson & Johnson can be found in many investor portfolios, for good reason. The company is an outstanding dividend stock. The company has paid a dividend every year since 1944 and has boosted its dividend in each of the last 47 years.

Tiny Titans

Dividend-paying stocks are usually large companies. However, a number of smaller companies offer attractive dividend payers. Two tiny dividend titans are Paychex (PAYX) and Buckle (BKE).

Paychex isn't exactly microscopic—the company's market capitalization is around $11 billion—but its size pales in comparison to lots of dividend payers. The company provides payroll-processing and human-resources administration for small and midsized companies. I own these shares and have generally been pleased with them over the years. The stock, yielding 4 percent, offers a nice balance of appreciation potential, dividend growth, and high current yield.

You may not be familiar with Buckle, but I bet your child or grandchild is. This retailer sells casual apparel, especially denim, for young men and women. Buckle sells those outrageously expensive jeans that are must-haves among teenagers and young adults. The company is that contradiction of sorts—a fast-growing firm with a fast-growing dividend and relatively high current yield. The stock yields nearly 3 percent. The dividend was initiated in 2003 and has increased more than fourfold since inception.

Nose Bleeds

I debated whether to include this next list of stocks. My fear is that readers will focus on these stocks because of their high yields. *Don't do that!* Build a portfolio of all sorts of dividend payers, not necessarily those with the highest yields. Many of the stocks with the highest yields are highly correlated, which means they tend to move in tandem. Constructing a portfolio exclusively of the names on the following list would leave you with a highly concentrated portfolio in stocks that, in some cases, have demonstrated lots of volatility in the last 24 months.

Furthermore, most of the stocks on this list are "pass-through" entities: that is, they don't pay taxes at the corporate level. Rather, cash flows and, in some cases, expenses and depreciation are passed through to the investor, who is responsible for paying the taxes. In most cases, these investments don't qualify for the 15 percent tax rate on dividends. You will be taxed at your ordinary tax rate on distributions and dividends. (I talk in greater depth about some of these "exotic" dividend investments in Chapter 8.)

———————— ～ ————————

Many of the stocks with the highest yields tend to move in tandem, which can leave your portfolio vulnerable to volatility.

To satisfy those investors who absolutely have to own stocks with high yields, the following "nose-bleed" stocks have super-high yields up to 12 percent, Advanced BSD scores of at least 63 (out of a possible 100), and Overall Quadrix scores of 60 and above.

Alliance Resource Partners LP (ARLP)

DCP Midstream Partners LP (DPM)

EV Energy Partners LP (EVEP)

Hi-Shear Technology (HSR)

Legacy Reserves LP (LGCY)

Linn Energy LLC (LINE)

Markwest Energy Partners LP (MWE)

Penn Virginia Res. Partners LP (PVR)

Suburban Propane Partners LP (SPH)

Sunoco Logistics Partners LP (SXL)

Get Out Your Passport: The 411 on ADRs

As I discussed at the beginning of this chapter, limiting yourself to U.S. stocks is unwise. More than two out of every three dollars invested in stocks globally is invested in companies outside the United States. Remember that when hunting for attractive dividend-paying stocks.

Diversification is the reason most often provided for investing overseas. There's some truth to that. International stocks don't correlate perfectly with U.S. stocks. However, 2008 demonstrated that this diversification may not work well during disastrous years. Indeed, the benchmark index for international stocks, the MSCI EAFE Index, declined some 45 percent in 2008, even worse than the decline in the Dow Jones Industrial Average and the S&P 500 Index. And some foreign countries saw their stock markets plunge 50 percent and 60 percent.

～

When you're hunting for attractive dividend-paying stocks, keep in mind that more than two out of every three dollars invested in stocks globally is invested in companies outside the United States.

I think a stronger argument for overseas investing is simply to expand your opportunity set—your fishing pond, if you well—for looking for potential winners.

The good news is that it has never been easier to invest overseas. Mutual funds have been the investment of choice for investors wanting to invest abroad. However, the growth of American Depositary Receipts (ADRs) has made it easier for U.S. investors to own individual foreign stocks. And the good news is that many quality foreign stocks pay handsome dividends.

ADRs are securities that trade on U.S. exchanges and represent ownership in shares of foreign companies. Investors buy and sell ADRs just as they buy and sell U.S. stocks. ADRs are quoted in U.S. dollars and pay dividends in U.S. dollars. And those dividend payments, in many cases, receive the preferential tax treatment (maximum 15 percent tax rate) afforded dividends paid by U.S. companies.

Overseas stocks usually pay dividends less frequently than U.S. companies, either annually or semiannually. Investors who require more regular cash flow may be turned off by the infrequent dividend payment schedules of ADRs. Also worth noting is that dividends will be impacted by currency exchange rates, so future dividends can fluctuate significantly. Finally, a portion of dividends paid on ADRs may be withheld for foreign tax purposes, although investors can recoup the money by filing for a foreign tax credit when they file their taxes. This foreign dividend tax issue may seem complicated. However, I have owned foreign dividend-paying stocks and can assure you that the tax implications of owning them are really no big deal.

Investing in ADRs exposes investors to some unique risks:

- *Currency risk.* During periods of a declining dollar, overseas firms generally benefit since their profits are puffed up when converted to weaker dollars. Conversely, a strong dollar usually crimps returns from foreign investments.

- *Political risk.* How foreign countries are governed can have a huge impact on the financial well-being of that country. Are the countries rooted in democracies and market-based solutions for economic and social problems? Or is political power concentrated in a ruling elite?

- *Volatile commodity prices.* Many countries, such as Russia, have commodity-dependent economies. In Russia's case, it's oil. If oil prices soar, Russian stocks usually do quite well. If oil prices tank, Russian stocks suffer. Commodity prices are volatile, which means that commodity-dependent economies and stock markets are volatile.

- *Unstable economic policies.* Hyperinflation has plagued many foreign countries over the years. While it can be argued that some emerging markets have done a better job of dealing with inflation in recent years, the risks of inflationary monetary policies still exist.

Jet Setters

The following list spotlights some of my favorite ADR dividend payers. Please note that all of these foreign stocks offer direct-purchase plans whereby any U.S. investor can buy ADRs directly from the company (or, more accurately, an agent of the company) without a broker. (I show you how to buy U.S. and ADR dividend payers directly in Chapter 5.)

AstraZeneca (AZN—United Kingdom)

China Life (LFC—China)

China Mobile (CHL—Hong Kong)

Fresenius Medical (FMS—Germany)

Infosys Technology (INFY—India)

Novartis (NVS—Switzerland)

Novo Nordisk (NVO—Denmark)

PetroChina (PTR—China)

Sanofi-Aventis (SNY—France)

SAP AG (SAP—Germany)

Smith & Nephew (SNN—United Kingdom)

Unilever PLC (UL—United Kingdom)

Among stocks in developed countries, I especially like AstraZeneca (AZN) and Novo Nordisk (NVO). Based in the United Kingdom, AstraZeneca is a leading pharmaceutical company. Top drugs include Crestor (cholesterol) and Symbicort (asthma). Novo Nordisk, based in Denmark, is the world's largest diabetes-care company. Given the rapid growth of diabetes throughout the world—the World Health Organization estimates the number of diabetics to exceed 350 million by 2030—Novo Nordisk should see continued demand for its products.

Building a Dividend Portfolio BRIC by BRIC

You'll notice that a few of my choices are situated in the "BRIC" countries—Brazil, Russia, India, and China. For long-term investors, BRIC countries offer plenty of appeal for a variety of reasons:

- The four BRIC countries account for more than 40 percent of the world's population.

- BRIC countries have growing middle classes with rising incomes. In 2002, BRIC countries had nearly 21 million households with annual disposable income above $10,000 (U.S.). By 2007, more than 90 million households exceeded the threshold. A vast and growing number of consumers and rapidly rising household incomes bode well for consumer spending, and that's great news for a host of BRIC stocks.

- When nearly all economies of developed countries were seeing declines in 2009, BRIC counties were seeing positive GDP growth.

- The political and economic instability that has historically plagued BRIC countries, while not completely gone, has certainly lessened. Brazil now carries an investment-grade rating on its debt. And the 2009 political victory by India's ruling Congress Party— a victory that was followed by a one-day gain in India's BSE Sensex index of 17 percent—and the world's positive response to China's $586 billion economic stimulus program illustrate the increasing comfort levels global investors have with BRIC financial, economic, and political policies.

- The continued weakness in the U.S. dollar, inflationary fears, and the desire for investors to generate higher returns in nondollar assets should boost BRIC stocks, many of which have big exposure to commodity and natural-resources markets.

While BRIC countries do have a lot going for them, it is worth noting that BRIC stocks also were crushed in 2008. Brazil's stock market declined 41 percent, Russia plummeted 72 percent, India dropped 52 percent, and China nosedived 65 percent. So stocks in these countries do carry their share of risk. Still, for investors who want to expand their fishing pond for dividend payers, BRIC stocks have appeal.

Among the BRIC dividend payers, I especially like China Mobile. Based in Hong Kong, China Mobile operates the world's largest mobile network with the world's largest mobile subscription base of more than 500 million subscribers. The company commands roughly 70 percent of the wireless market in China. The stock yields more than 3 percent, and I expect regular dividend increases to continue.

Yield!

- *All shapes and sizes welcome.* When buying big, safe dividend stocks, make sure to include large, midsized, and small stocks. You'll improve portfolio diversification.

- *Don't forget your passport.* Some of the best dividend stocks are located outside the U.S. It's never been easier to buy them via ADRs.

- *Frisky for risky? Take a chill pill.* It's okay to include a few super-high yielders in a dividend portfolio. But remember that such stocks tend to move in tandem, which reduces portfolio diversification and increases risk.

Chapter Five

It Pays to Be Direct

Save Money by Buying Dividend
Stocks Direct

I BOUGHT SHARES IN OIL GIANT EXXON IN APRIL 1992. At the time, Exxon stock was trading for $58.54 per share. (Adjusted for subsequent stock splits, my cost basis is $14.63, so I've done pretty well on my initial investment.)

That I bought Exxon probably doesn't shock you. Exxon was and still is a top-notch investment, one that has typically been popular with individual investors, especially those who like dividends. The firm is an elite company when it comes to the dividend. Exxon has paid a dividend every year since 1882 and has boosted its dividend annually for the last 27 years.

How I bought Exxon, however, may surprise you. I didn't buy Exxon through a stock broker. (I actually didn't have a regular broker in 1992.) And I didn't invest $5,854 to buy 100 shares of stock (many investors like to buy round lots of 100 shares).

I bought the stock directly from the company, without a broker. And I only put up $250, which bought me 4.27 shares of Exxon. That's right—I bought full *and* fractional shares of the stock, and best of all, I didn't pay a penny in trading fees to buy my Exxon stock. All of my money went to work for me.

Ever since 1992, I've continued to buy Exxon stock. Sometimes, I invested just $100. Sometimes I invested $200 or $500. One time, I even invested just $3.07 to buy 0.049 shares of stock. But every time I bought Exxon stock, I never used a stock broker, and I never paid a trading commission. I went direct, for free.

This wasn't some special deal I had with Exxon. Any investor can buy shares directly, without a broker and without paying any fees. You could back in 1992. And you can today.

Why You Should Buy Direct

Buying big, safe dividend stocks is important, but most investors don't give it much thought.

You should.

How you buy your investments, and the fees you incur to buy stock, has a direct impact on your returns. It's fair to say that every dollar you pay to buy stock is one less dollar in cash flows generated by your investment. In a way, that's a direct offset to your dividend stream.

When I first started in the business, it wasn't unusual for investors to pay $100 or more to buy 100 shares of stock at some full-service brokers. Paying such high commissions represented a major drag on returns for investors. If you bought 100 shares of a $30 stock, your investment was $3,000 plus commissions, which may have been $125 in the early 1980s. That trading fee represented 4.1 percent of your initial investment. Let's assume the stock you bought had a yield of 4.0 percent, which means you received $120 in dividends the first year. The bad news is that the $125 in trading fees effectively wiped out one year's worth of dividends. To put it a different way, your first-year dividend yield was effectively *zero* (actually, it was less than zero) when you factored in trading fees.

———————————— ∼ ————————————

**Every dollar you pay to buy stock is
one less dollar in cash flows generated
by your investment.**

————————————————————————————

Fortunately, trading fees have come down considerably in the last 25 years. Today, you can buy 100 shares of stock at many discount brokers for less than $15 per trade.

However, even modest trading fees can have a noticeable impact on returns. This impact is accentuated in low-yield environments. If the yield on your portfolio is 2 percent, losing 0.2 percent per year to trading fees—which is easy to do even when paying very low commissions—in effect reduces your cash flow by 10 percent (0.2 percent divided by 2 percent).

And if you are someone who likes to "dollar-cost average"—making investments on a regular basis, perhaps monthly—even modest trading fees can add up big time. Let's say you buy every month. Even if you are paying just $10 per trade, that commission adds up to $120 per year for just one stock. Multiply that over 5 or 10 stocks, and you could be looking at $600 to more than $1,000 per year in commissions. That's $1,000 that will never go towards a car payment, rent check, or any of the other million expenses we all have. It's gone forever.

How You Can Buy Stocks Direct

When I bought my Exxon stock in 1992, I didn't pay any brokerage fees. That's because I didn't use a broker. I purchased the stock via Exxon's direct-stock purchase plan.

Direct-stock purchase plans are an offshoot of Dividend Reinvestment Plans (DRIPs), which are offered by more than 1,000 companies. These are programs that allow investors to buy stock directly from companies. Shares are purchased in two ways:

1. **Reinvested dividends.** Instead of receiving a dividend check, DRIP investors have the company reinvest those dividends to buy more shares of stock.
2. **Optional cash investments.** Once enrolled in a DRIP, investors may make optional investments whereby they send money directly to the company (or, more likely, an agent of the company, known as a transfer agent, which administers the DRIP on the company's behalf) to buy additional shares.

DRIPs, which I discuss at length in Chapter 9, appeal to investors for several reasons. In most cases, investment minimums are quite small; usually less than $250 and often below $100. This makes it affordable for anyone, even those with tiny pocketbooks, to buy stock. Second, full and fractional shares are purchased. If a stock trades for $50 per share and you invest $25, you'll buy half a share of stock. That half of a share is entitled to half the dividend. Think of it as buying stock on the installment plan.

Another big attraction of DRIPs is that the fees to buy shares are modest. In most cases, you'll pay less than $5 per purchase. And in many plans, the trading fees are zero.

While DRIPs have a lot to offer investors, there is a catch: how you get into the plans in the first place. Many DRIPs require you to be a shareholder of record already, before you can participate in the plan. As a shareholder of record, the stock is registered in your name and not in the name of the broker or "street" name.

So how do you get that first share? It's not always as easy as it sounds. You may not have enough money to open a brokerage account, or you may feel sheepish going to a broker and buying just one share.

Many companies have simplified the process by creating plans that allow any investor to *buy the first share and every share directly from the company*. These plans are often referred to as direct-purchase plans; I call them "no-load stocks" because the plans are similar to no-load mutual funds whereby an investor buys fund shares directly from the fund, without a broker and often without purchase fees.

I made my initial purchase of Exxon back in 1992 via the company's direct-purchase plan. At that time Exxon was one of only a handful of companies offering the option to buy the first share and every share directly. Over time, however, the number of companies has grown dramatically. Today, more than 350 U.S. companies allow investors to buy stock directly, without a broker. And many of these companies are among some of the best dividend-paying stocks in the market.

Twenty-two of the 30 stocks in the Dow Jones Industrial Average offer direct-purchase plans, including such strong dividend payers as Procter & Gamble and Coca-Cola. (Procter & Gamble has paid a dividend since 1891 and has boosted its dividend annually for more than 50 years. Coca-Cola has paid a dividend continuously since 1893 and has increased its dividend in each of the last 47 years.)

Direct-purchase plans are not limited to U.S. companies. More than 250 international companies whose American Depositary Receipts (ADRs) trade on U.S. stock exchanges allow investors to buy shares directly— the first share and every share. Many of these ADR direct-purchase plans include solid dividend-paying stocks, including Novartis (a Swiss-based pharmaceutical company) and Danish-based Novo Nordisk (the world's leading provider of treatments for diabetes).

Direct-purchase plans make it very easy for investors to make the initial investment as well as subsequent investments. Just follow these steps.

Contact the Company

Virtually all direct-purchase plans have toll-free numbers to call to obtain the necessary plan brochure and enrollment information. Alternatively, you can obtain enrollment information online by going to company or transfer agent web sites. Transfer agents are entities companies hire to administer their plans. Major transfer agents include:

Computershare: www.computershare.com

BNY Mellon: www.stockbny.com

Wells Fargo Shareowner Services:
    www.shareowneronline.com

American Stock Transfer and Trust: www.amstock.com

JP Morgan: www.adr.com

Citibank: www.citibank.com/adr

Deutsche Bank: www.adr.db.com

Registrar and Transfer Co.: www.rtco.com

Read the Plan Brochure

Not all direct-purchase plans are the same. For example, more than half of all direct-purchase plans have initial minimums of $250 or less. However, some have initial minimums of $1,000. Some plans waive their minimum initial investment if an investor agrees to monthly automatic investments via electronic debit of a bank account. Some plans charge fees on the buy side, while others do not. And some plans have special features. For example, Exxon and Wal-Mart have IRA options, including the Roth IRA, built directly into the direct-purchase plans. To ensure that there are no surprises, read the plan brochure that accompanies the enrollment information.

Make Your Initial Investment

Once you have decided on a company, cut a check and return it with your completed enrollment form to the company or its agent. If you prefer, you can also make initial investments in a host of direct-purchase plans by going to their transfer agent web sites and investing online.

Keep Records

It is important to maintain a record of your investments. Having records and statements will make it easier to compute your cost basis for tax purposes should you sell your shares.

Once you have made your initial investment, you will receive a statement from the transfer agent. This statement will show the amount and cost of the shares purchased.

You will not receive the actual stock certificates unless you request them. Your shares will be recorded in book-entry format known as "direct registration."

Lather, Rinse, and Repeat

Once in the plan, you can invest in two ways: by reinvesting your dividends and by making "optional cash investments" directly to the plan.

Optional cash investments are just that—optional. You are not required to make additional investments, but part of the power of these plans is the ability to make ongoing investments in a low-cost or even no-cost way. In most cases, the minimum subsequent investment in these plans is $50 or less.

Should You or Shouldn't You?

Are direct-purchase plans perfect for every investor? I'm not sure an investment vehicle exists that is perfect for every investor. Direct-purchase plans come pretty close, especially for newcomers to the stock market or those with limited investment funds. Still, there are aspects of the plans that you need to understand in order to judge whether they make sense for you.

- *You can't control the buy price.* When buying in these plans, you don't have the precision over the purchase price that you have through a broker. If you want to buy stock *right now*, you can't do that with these plans. Companies may buy shares only once a week. I participate in several direct-purchase plans, and this delay on the buy side has never been much of a problem since I'm not trading these stocks. Still, for investors who want precise control over the buy price, these plans may not be that attractive. The plans are best used by investors who want to buy and build a stock position over time, not trading in and out.

- *They require a certain amount of record-keeping.* When you buy shares through a stock broker, you receive one consolidated statement showing all of your holdings. There is no such thing as a consolidated statement in direct-purchase plans. You are dealing with each company one-on-one. If you are in five direct-purchase plans, you will receive statements from each of the five companies. I can tell you first hand that, as long as you keep these statements, record-keeping hassles are fairly limited. Still, for investors who like the simplicity of a consolidated statement, these plans may not be for them.

- *Some plans involve fees.* Although many plans charge no fees on the buy side, a growing number of direct-purchase plans have implemented fees to purchase shares. These fees may include a one-time enrollment fee of $5 to $15 as well as ongoing purchase fees. The ongoing purchase fees are usually much lower than what you would pay even through the cheapest online broker—usually $5 or less. Still, some plans do have purchase fees that investors may consider excessive. Also, selling fees—and you can sell your shares through these plans as well as buy—may be $20 or more. If you find the selling fees are more expensive than selling through your broker, you can always transfer the shares from the direct-purchase plan to your brokerage account and then sell the shares through the broker.

A Starter Portfolio for Your Kid, or Your Grandkid, or Yourself

Direct-purchase plans allow any investor—young or old, rich or not-so-rich—to buy quality stocks in amounts that make sense for their situation.

While this book is meant for anyone looking to take advantage of what dividend investing has to offer, children possess that ingredient that is most important in producing big investment returns: time.

Direct-purchase plans are the perfect vehicles for introducing a young person to stocks. Most direct-purchase plans can be set up as UGMA (Uniform Gifts to Minors Act) custodial accounts. Alternatively, a parent or grandparent can open up a direct-purchase plan in the parent or grandparent's name and mentally earmark the account for the child. Best of all, a number of direct-purchase plans are offered by companies that may have special appeal to young people.

To find stocks that represent especially interesting plays for young investors, I culled the list of direct-purchase plans for those with minimum initial investments of $100 or less. I figured that such a low investment amount falls more closely into that "gift" category of $100, making direct-purchase plans a great idea for a birthday or graduation gift. A low minimum initial investment also makes it more likely that the kids will kick in a few bucks of their own.

—————————— ∽ ——————————

Young investors possess the most important ingredient in producing big returns: time.

Next, I narrowed the list to companies a young investor may be familiar with.

What fell out of my search were the following three companies:

1. **CVS Caremark** is a leading drugstore chain and pharmacy benefits manager. Long-term growth in profits and dividends should be in the 6 to 11 percent

range. I think CVS should be one of the winners as access to health care is expanded. Given CVS's national brand, the stock may have special appeal for a youngster who is familiar with the stores. CVS's minimum initial investment is $100. For enrollment information and a plan prospectus call (877) 287-7526.

2. **FPL Group,** through its utility operations, services more than 4 million residential, commercial, and industrial customers in Florida. The firm is also a major player in alternative energy. In fact, the company's NextEra Energy Resources unit is the No. 1 wind energy company in the United States and is the nation's leading operator of solar-power generation. The green activities of FPL may be especially appealing to young investors. FPL ranks as one of the more attractive utilities in the market. The company has increased its dividend for 14 consecutive years. Minimum initial investment in the company's direct-purchase plan is $100. For enrollment information and a prospectus call (888) 218-4392.

3. Who isn't familiar with **Kellogg**? The company is the world's leading producer of cereal and a leading producer of convenience foods,

including cookies, crackers, toaster pastries, cereal bars, frozen waffles, and meat alternatives. Brands include Kellogg's, Pop-Tarts, Eggo, Cheez-It, Club, Gardenburger, Nutri-Grain, Rice Krispies, Special K, Mini-Wheats, Morningstar Farms, and Famous Amos. The company has paid a dividend for more than 80 years. Minimum initial investment in Kellogg's direct-purchase plan is just $50. For enrollment information and a plan prospectus call (877) 910-5385.

To make initial investments in the stocks in this three-stock "Starter Portfolio" requires a total cash outlay of just $250. Note that all three have stable and rising dividend streams.

Selling young investors on the benefits of investing should be pretty easy. Just show them the money. Remember the story I told you at the beginning of this book about how I wished I had bought Exxon when I was just starting my working career? What if I had bought Exxon stock when I was a teenager?

A $100 investment in Exxon on September 28, 1973 (the day I turned 13) would be worth $14,800. ("Not too shabby . . .")

A $1,000 investment would have me sitting on
$148,000. ("That sounds even better . . .")

A $10,000 investment means I'd currently own Exxon
stock worth *$1.48 million.* ("Where do I sign up?")

That should get their attention.

Top Direct-Purchase Plans for Dividend Investors

Following is a sampling of some of my favorite dividend-
paying U.S. and international companies offering direct-
purchase plans. The list includes the contact numbers to
obtain the enrollment information, along with the minimum
initial investments required in the plans. For a complete
list of all U.S. and international direct-purchase plans,
visit our free web site at www.bigsafedividends.com.

Company (Ticker)	Minimum Initial Investment	Phone Number
Aflac (AFL)	$1,000	800-235-2667
AGL Resources (AGL)	$ 250	800-468-9716
Aqua America (WTR)	$ 500	800-205-8314
AstraZeneca PLC (AZN) (United Kingdom)	$ 250	800-428-4237
Bristol-Myers Squibb (BMY)	$ 250	800-356-2026
China Mobile (CHL) (Hong Kong)	$ 200	800-345-1612
Coca-Cola (KO)	$ 500	888-265-3747

Company (Ticker)	Minimum Initial Investment	Phone Number
Cracker Barrel (CBRL)	$250	800-278-4353
CVS Caremark (CVS)	$100	877-287-7526
Disney (DIS)	$250	818-553-7200
Eaton (ETN)	$100	866-353-7849
Emerson Electric (EMR)	$250	866-353-7849
Entertainment Prop. (EPR)	$200	800-884-4225
Exxon Mobil (XOM)	$250	800-252-1800
FPL Group (FPL)	$100	888-218-4392
Fresenius Medical (FMS) (Germany)	$200	800-345-1612
General Mills (GIS)	$250	800-670-4763
IBM (IBM)	$500	888-426-6700
Kellogg (K)	$ 50	877-910-5385
McDonald's (MCD)	$500	800-621-7825
Medtronic (MDT)	$250	888-648-8154
Microsoft (MSFT)	$250	800-285-7772
Novartis (NVS) (Switzerland)	$500	800-428-4237
Novo Nordisk A/S (NVO) (Denmark)	$250	800-428-4237
Paychex (PAYX)	$250	877-814-9688
PepsiCo (PEP)	$250	800-226-0083
PetroChina (PTR) (China)	$200	800-345-1612
Petroleo Brasileiro (PBR) (Brazil)	$250	800-428-4237
Philip Morris Int'l (PM)	$500	877-745-9350
Procter & Gamble (PG)	$250	800-742-6253
Walgreen (WAG)	$250	888-368-7346
Wal-Mart Stores (WMT)	$250	800-438-6278

Yield!

- *No excuses*. With direct-purchase plans, any investor has an easy and affordable way to buy quality dividend stocks.

- *No fee means more dividend cash in your pocket*. Want to know a *guaranteed* way to boost investment returns? Reduce or eliminate transaction costs with direct-purchase plans.

- *No height requirement*. Young investors can start building serious wealth via direct-purchase plans. All it takes is $50 to buy attractive dividend payers.

Chapter Six

Postcards from the Hedge

~

Beat Inflation—and the Stock Market—with Dividend Growers

WHAT IS PUBLIC ENEMY No. 1 for income investors?

The answers may vary in specifics, but you will find a common thread: *they all involve the loss of purchasing power, otherwise known as inflation.*

How devastating can inflation be to your nest egg? Let's look at a simple example. If inflation averages

3 percent per year, in 12 years, the purchasing power of your cash flows is cut by 30 percent. That means that a person who retires at age 62 will see his purchasing power decline by 30 cents for every dollar of cash flow by age 74.

By age 86, the purchasing power will be cut in half. In a nutshell: At an inflation rate of just 3 percent per year, $1 today will Be worth just 50 cents in less than 25 years.

Here's an easy way to understand the relationship of inflation and purchasing power. Let's say your local grocer sells a loaf of bread for $1.50. If the price increases 3 percent per year, 25 years from now that loaf of bread will cost more than $3. If you currently allocate $5 per month for bread purchases (and, yes, I know most people don't have "bread" as a line item on their monthly budget, but indulge me here), you'll buy about half as much bread 25 years from now with that $5. In effect, your bread purchasing power has been cut in half because of the 3 percent per year price increases.

It is easy to ignore the effects of inflation on future cash flows; an annual cash flow of, say, $100,000 sounds pretty good if you are at or near retirement. But if that $100,000 stagnates and doesn't grow, its real value 25 years from now will be less than $50,000.

How can income investors fight inflation? *Own investments that pay higher income every year.*

You Need to Growth Up

One way to hedge against inflation is to focus on stocks that are likely to boost their dividends on a regular basis. The math is simple, but compelling. If a stock pays you dividends of $200 per year, and the dividend increases 3 percent per year, you'll receive more than $400 in dividends from that stock 25 years from now. Returning to our bread example, the percentage growth in your dividend kept pace with the percentage growth in the price of a loaf of bread. You suffered no loss of purchasing power.

The bottom line is that if your dividends can at least keep pace with inflation—and hopefully exceed the inflation rate—your real spending power can be maintained or increased over time.

Dividend growth may be the best friend of income investors, but it's often overlooked because income investors focus on today (current yield) and not tomorrow (dividend growth). That's a mistake, especially if you buy and hold stocks for long periods of time.

～

One way to hedge against inflation is to focus on stocks that are likely to boost their dividends on a regular basis.

I'm not saying that finding stocks that increase their dividends every year is a slam dunk. It certainly wasn't in the third quarter of 2009. According to Standard & Poor's, only 191 companies increased their dividend payments during the quarter. It was the worst third quarter in history for dividend increases.

Even so, for investors who find consistent dividend growers, the fruits are ample. You'll beat inflation, you'll achieve quicker payback on your initial investment (I'll get to the concept of payback later in the chapter), and, best of all, you'll increase your chances of owning stocks with attractive capital-gains potential.

You Can't Eat Yield

You can't buy stuff or pay your bills with yield. You buy stuff and pay your bills with *dollars*.

That's why this book's title is *The Little Book of Big Dividends*, not *The Little Book of Big Yields*. You don't necessarily need big yields to generate big dividends. In fact, in many cases the biggest dividends over time come from moderate yielders that grow their dividends regularly.

So, why do income investors focus on yield instead of actual dollars?

I think part of the reason stems from the way individuals typically frame buying decisions. We think in percentage terms and often ignore the dollar implications. For example, many people will drive across town to save $2 on a gallon of milk. (If you don't believe me, talk to a manager of any grocery store.) On the other hand, few consumers would drive across town to save $2 on an auto purchase—same $2, different percentages. A $2 discount on a gallon of milk may be a 65 percent savings. A $2 savings on a $30,000 auto purchase is 0.0066 percent.

I can't tell you how many times investors have told me about moving money from one investment to a more risky investment in order to generate an extra 1 percent yield. I'm all for squeezing out as much return as possible from your hard-earned money, but too often bad decisions are made in the name of higher yields. Remember that yield is a good proxy for risk. When you move money to a higher-yielding investment, it's likely you are moving to a higher-risk investment.

Say an investor wants to move money from a federally-insured bank account to an uninsured money market account. The person may get an extra 0.5 percent or 1.0 percent yield bump by moving to the money market. Good idea? Perhaps. But what I tell people is don't think in terms of the yield. Think in terms of the actual dollars gained. If the amount of money involved is $5,000, the additional 1 percent is just $50. Do you want to move money from an insured account to an uninsured account—even if the chances of problems are very remote—for just $50?

Wall Streeters have an expression for this investor mentality. They call it "picking up nickels in front of a steamroller." You can make a few extra bucks, but if something goes wrong, you will be crushed.

A good example of the dangers of picking up nickels in front of a steamroller was the auction-rate-securities debacle of 2008 and 2009. Auction-rate securities were sold as "almost as safe as Treasuries and money markets, but with higher yields." The yields were higher, but not by much, and the risks turned out to be much greater than money markets and Treasuries. Investors found out about these risks when the market for auction-rate securities imploded during the credit crisis in 2008 and early 2009. Investment firms stopped supporting the market. The result was that the market for auction-rate securities seized up, effectively locking out investors from selling their investments and getting their cash.

Reading the Tea Leaves

Since dividends are paid with cash, they can't be faked. They can't be created through accounting magic; either you pay the dividend, or you don't.

When a company makes a commitment to pay the dividend, it's showing confidence that it will be able to continue to pay this commitment to shareholders.

When a company *increases* its dividend, the firm is saying that it believes the company's future is strong enough to support an increase in shareholder cash flows. Such decisions are not made lightly. The last thing a company wants to do is raise the dividend in one quarter only to cut or omit the dividend in subsequent quarters.

A dividend increase is not a perfect signal that the future is bright. Just ask the banks that boosted dividends in 2006 and 2007 only to fall into the abyss in 2008.

Still, as an investor, you play percentages. And the percentages say that under most circumstances a company is not likely to raise its dividend without having a high degree of confidence that it can deliver.

For example, amid perhaps the worst period ever for dividend cuts and omissions, Abbot Laboratories raised its dividend 11 percent in early 2008 and again in early 2009. Abbott's confidence in its future was well placed. The company posted solid profit growth in 2008 and 2009.

That confidence in the future also manifested itself in superior stock price performance. Abbott stock fell in 2008 along with just about every other stock. Abbott's decline, however, was just 5 percent for the year.

Not bad considering that the Dow Jones Industrial Average plummeted nearly 34 percent in 2008.

We ran a study of all stocks in the S&P 1500 that boosted their dividends each year going back to the end of 1994. What we found was that, as a group, companies that boosted their dividends outperformed—by nearly 2 percent per year—those that didn't boost their dividend. And they generated those higher returns at lower risk as measured by standard deviation of returns. Even more impressive, dividend growers outperformed the broad market, as measured by the S&P 1500 Index, by about 2 percent per year on average.

The moral of the story: Buying dividend growers is not just a good idea as an inflation hedge. It's a good idea because dividend growers, as a group, outperform the market.

Buying dividend growers is not just a good idea as an inflation hedge; it's a good idea because dividend growers, as a group, outperform the market.

The Age-Old Question: Risk vs. Reward

Let's say you buy 200 shares of a $40 stock. Your investment is $8,000. And let's say the stock pays a dividend of $1.20 per share (that's a yield of 3 percent). Based on that dividend, you expect to receive $240 in dividends the first year. If that dividend stream never changes, you will recoup your initial $8,000 investment in roughly 33 years. I call that your *payback*.

Depending on your age, 33 years may actually be a legitimate holding period for your investments. I know investors who have held stocks for 30 years or more who have become rich by owning those stocks.

Still, 33 years is a fairly long period of time to recoup an investment.

What if that dividend stream grew just 3 percent per year instead of staying stagnant?

You would recoup your initial $8,000 investment via dividend payments in less than 24 years.

And what if that dividend stream grew at 5 percent per year?

You would recoup your initial investment in 20 years.

This calculation is not affected by the movement of the stock price over time. It isn't impacted by the stock's yield over time. It only makes one assumption—expected dividend growth—to compute the length of time to recoup your initial investment.

Think of payback as a safety-net approach to stock investing. Obviously, nobody knows for sure how a stock is going to behave over time. The hope, of course, is that it doesn't go bust, that it maintains and grows its dividend, and that you can make a few extra bucks in terms of price appreciation. By calculating a payback period, you help establish an expected baseline performance, kind of a worst-case scenario, for getting your initial investment back.

Most investors look at two stocks and select the one they believe has the most upside over time. This places all the focus on reward. Calculating a stock's payback based on dividend flow forces you to address the following question: If this stock never makes me any money in terms of price appreciation, how long would it take for the dividend payments to bail me out of my initial investment?

Should you focus on stocks that have the quickest payback? Not necessarily. Ultimately, total return is what matters. It's great to have a stock pay back your initial investment in just 15 years, but it's a whole lot better to own a stock that increases your initial investment fivefold in 15 years.

Still, using dividend payback is a worthwhile concept for framing the risk-return potential of two stocks. It's also a useful tie-breaker when choosing between two investments.

Exhibit 6.1 provides a matrix to help you determine payback times based on dividend yields and dividend-growth assumptions. For example, a stock that yields 4 percent and boosts its dividend 6 percent per year has a dividend payback of 16 years.

Exhibit 6.1 Dividend Payback Matrix

		Dividend Yield				
		2%	3%	4%	5%	6%
Dividend Growth Rate	0%	50	33	25	20	17
	3	31	23	19	16	14
	4	28	22	18	15	13
	5	26	20	17	14	12
	6	24	19	16	13	12
	7	22	18	15	13	12
	8	21	17	14	12	11
	9	20	16	14	12	10
	10	19	15	13	11	10

Use the Advanced BSD Formula to Find Growers

An excellent way to zero in on dividend growers is to use the Advanced BSD formula (detailed in Appendix A). Companies that have high BSD scores typically have excellent dividend-growth prospects. That's because the Advanced BSD formula factors in the most important components of dividend growth:

- Profit growth
- Cash-flow growth
- Payout ratio

Profits and cash flow ultimately determine the amount of dividends a company can pay; if profits and cash flow are rising, dividends should follow. The payout ratio shows the amount of flexibility a company has with its dividend.

A payout ratio of 60 percent ($1 in dividends paid out for every $1.66 in profits) or below reflects a company that is more likely to maintain or boost its dividend than one already paying out most of its profits in dividends.

It's also useful to match up companies with strong BSD scores with firms that have a history of boosting their dividend on an annual basis. Past is not always pro-logue, but companies that have demonstrated a willingness and ability to increase their dividend each year are good bets to continue to boost dividends. (Remember, you can get up-to-date BSD scores on all the dividend-paying stocks in the S&P 1500 at www.bigsafedividends.com.)

The 10/10 Club

For investors searching for consistent dividend growers, the following stocks should fit the bill.

Aflac (AFL)

Automatic Data Processing (ADP)

Colgate-Palmolive (CL)

Johnson & Johnson (JNJ)

Medtronic (MDT)

PepsiCo (PEP)

United Technologies (UTX)

Wal-Mart Stores (WMT)

These stocks, all with Advanced BSD and Quadrix scores of at least 70, meet the following criteria:

- Higher dividends every year for at least 10 years
- Annual dividend growth averaging at least 10 percent over the last 10 years

Finish Strong

In racing parlance, current yield is only the starting line. And as everyone knows, it's not how you start a race, it's how you finish. Dividend growth hedges against inflation, accelerates your payback on investment, and tends to point you toward stocks that beat the market—three things that will help you cross the finish line a winner.

Yield!

- *Hedge me if you can.* Higher dividends are a great inflation hedge.
- *Payback is a pitch for dividend growers.* Dividend growth accelerates the payback on your investment.
- *Put on your signal.* Companies that increase their dividends signal their confidence in the future—a confidence that should manifest itself in market-beating returns.

Lifeguard on Duty

*Strategies for Draining the Pool
without Outlasting Your Money*

You spend the bulk of your life building wealth. But what about when you need to start drawing on those funds? What's the best way to pay yourself while making sure your money lasts as long as you do?

The best withdrawal rate (I call this "draining the pool") is a hot topic. As with most complicated questions, there is no one-size-fits-all answer. An individual retiring at age 72—for whom the Internal Revenue Service projects a life expectancy of 15.5 years—may opt for a more aggressive withdrawal strategy than an individual retiring at age 55 with a life expectancy of nearly 30 years. Portfolio size and income needs will also impact the size of your withdrawals.

At the heart of this issue lies a fear of any retiree—the fear of outliving your funds. Research suggests that an initial withdrawal rate of 3 to 4 percent, with an asset allocation of 50 to 75 percent in stocks and the remainder in bonds and cash, gives you the best chance of fully funding your retirement.

Making Your Nest Egg Last

Let's look at an example. Say your retirement nest egg is $500,000. Your initial withdrawal in year one should be in the range of $15,000 to $20,000 (3 or 4 percent of $500,000). In year two, your withdrawal rate is $15,450 to $20,600 (year one withdrawal plus 3 percent inflation). And so on.

Notice that in this example your withdrawal rates are not affected by investment returns, at least initially. However, the performance of your investments over time could influence your withdrawal amounts.

The initial 3 to 4 percent withdrawal rule is based to a large extent on historical average market returns. But your actual investment returns may be anything *but* average (remember 2008?). That's the nightmare of any withdrawal plan—unusually large market declines, especially in the early years of retirement.

How would three ugly years in the market affect this withdrawal strategy? Exhibit 7.1 shows how a portfolio would fare assuming a 3 percent initial withdrawal rate and 3 percent annual increases to reflect inflation. In the example, we take a worst-case approach and build in a 17 percent decline in portfolio value in each of the first three years of retirement. (If you assume a 60/40 split in stocks versus bonds, a 17 percent decline would represent a significant annual drop in portfolio value. Such a decline for three consecutive years would be highly unusual.) Following those three years of declines, investment returns average 4.5 percent per year.

As you see, the $500,000 portfolio is down nearly 50 percent after year three. However, even with that initial shock, the portfolio lasts 20 years. And remember, the example assumes that you bump your annual withdrawal 3 percent to take into account inflation.

Bottom line: Consider an initial 3 to 4 percent withdrawal rate, especially if you expect to live 20 years or more. If your investments do well in the early years of retirement, you can increase your withdrawal rate. Conversely, you can adjust your withdrawals downward if early returns are poor.

Exhibit 7.1 Takes a Lickin' and Keeps on Tickin'

Year	Starting Portfolio Value	3% Initial Withdrawal; 3% Annual Inflation	Annual Return	Ending Portfolio Value
1	$500,000	$15,000	−17.0%	$402,550
2	$402,550	$15,450	−17.0%	$321,293
3	$321,293	$15,914	−17.0%	$253,465
4	$253,465	$16,391	4.5%	$247,742
5	$247,742	$16,883	4.5%	$241,248
6	$241,248	$17,389	4.5%	$233,933
7	$233,933	$17,911	4.5%	$225,743
8	$225,743	$18,448	4.5%	$216,623
9	$216,623	$19,002	4.5%	$206,515
10	$206,515	$19,572	4.5%	$195,356
11	$195,356	$20,159	4.5%	$183,081
12	$183,081	$20,764	4.5%	$169,622
13	$169,622	$21,386	4.5%	$154,906
14	$154,906	$22,028	4.5%	$138,857
15	$138,857	$22,689	4.5%	$121,396
16	$121,396	$23,370	4.5%	$102,438
17	$102,438	$24,071	4.5%	$ 81,894
18	$ 81,894	$24,793	4.5%	$ 59,670
19	$ 59,670	$25,536	4.5%	$ 35,670
20	$ 35,670	$26,303	4.5%	$ 9,789

～

Consider an initial 3 to 4 percent withdrawal
rate, especially if you expect to live
20 years or more.

Creating Your Own Income

You can generate cash flow from a portfolio in a couple of ways. You can generate cash by taking the dividends and income produced by your investments. You can generate cash by selling stocks. Most investors focus on the former. Smart investors focus on both.

It goes back to a primary message of this book: *Total return—dividends plus capital gains—is what truly matters when selecting investments.*

Wouldn't you rather have a stock that produces a total return of 15 percent (even if the dividend yield is only 2 percent) versus a stock that produces a total return of 10 percent (even if the yield is 5 percent)? You have more money with the first stock, which means you have more money from which to generate cash if you need it.

In short, you always want your portfolio to show the maximum increase in *total value*. The best way to generate that increase in value is to buy stocks with solid potential for both capital gains and dividend growth. If you limit your selections to high-yielding stocks, most of which have only modest appreciation potential, you limit your total-return potential and consequently, your ability to generate cash flows from your portfolio.

[98] THE LITTLE BOOK OF BIG DIVIDENDS

Here's an example that shows how maximizing total return is the optimal approach for producing cash flow. Exhibit 7.2 shows two portfolios. Portfolio A yields 5 percent, but portfolio appreciation averages just 3 percent per year for an annual total return of 8 percent. Portfolio B has a much smaller yield of 2 percent but appreciation of 8 percent per year for an annual total return of 10 percent.

Cash flows listed in the table assume that Portfolio A pays out 5 percent of its value in dividends each year, while the investor with Portfolio B collects dividends equal to 2 percent of the portfolio value and sells stock at the end of each year equal to 3 percent of the portfolio value. (Long-term capital gains—profits on stocks held more than 12 months—and dividends are currently taxed at the same maximum rate of 15 percent, so there is no tax advantage between generating cash flow from dividends or from selling stocks with long-term capital gains.)

As the table shows, a portfolio with a modest yield and decent appreciation potential can deliver higher cash flows (as well as more principal growth) than a portfolio with a high yield but more modest appreciation—provided you're willing to sell stocks to raise the cash flow you need.

Portfolio B has a value after 20 years of more than $253,000, 40 percent higher than the value of Portfolio A.

Exhibit 7.2 Creating Your Own Income

	Portfolio A Yields 5%, with Capital Gains of 3%			Portfolio B Yields 2%, with Capital Gains of 8%			
	Value	Cash Flow		Value	Yield	Sale of Stock	Cash Flow
Year 1	$100,000	$5,000	Year 1	$100,000	$2,000	$3,240	$5,240
Year 2	103,000	5,150	Year 2	104,760	2,095	3,394	5,489
Year 3	106,090	5,305	Year 3	109,747	2,195	3,556	5,751
Year 4	109,273	5,464	Year 4	114,971	2,299	3,725	6,024
Year 5	112,551	5,628	Year 5	120,443	2,409	3,902	6,311
Year 6	115,927	5,796	Year 6	126,176	2,524	4,088	6,612
Year 7	119,405	5,970	Year 7	132,182	2,644	4,283	6,927
Year 8	122,987	6,149	Year 8	138,474	2,769	4,487	7,256
Year 9	126,677	6,334	Year 9	145,065	2,901	4,700	7,601
Year 10	130,477	6,524	Year 10	151,971	3,039	4,924	7,963
Year 11	134,392	6,720	Year 11	159,204	3,184	5,158	8,342
Year 12	138,423	6,921	Year 12	166,782	3,336	5,404	8,740
Year 13	142,576	7,129	Year 13	174,721	3,494	5,661	9,155
Year 14	146,853	7,343	Year 14	183,038	3,661	5,930	9,591
Year 15	151,259	7,563	Year 15	191,751	3,835	6,213	10,048
Year 16	155,797	7,790	Year 16	200,878	4,018	6,508	10,526
Year 17	160,471	8,024	Year 17	210,440	4,209	6,818	11,027
Year 18	165,285	8,264	Year 18	220,457	4,409	7,143	11,552
Year 19	170,243	8,512	Year 19	230,950	4,619	7,483	12,102
Year 20	175,351	8,768	Year 20	241,944	4,839	7,839	12,678

What's more, annual cash flows thrown off from Portfolio B are consistently higher than those of Portfolio B. In year 20, for example, Portfolio B's cash flow of more than $12,600 is 44 percent higher than Portfolio A.

Am I twisting returns a bit here to create my desired outcome? Sure. Obviously, if Portfolio B is generating 2 percent per year more in total returns, the outcome is going to be better for Portfolio B than Portfolio A. *But that's my point.* It's total return that should matter to income investors, not current yield. A 5 percent yielder is not better than a 2 percent yielder if the 2 percent yielder consistently generates higher total returns.

Is it a guarantee that all 2 percent yielders will out-perform 5 percent yielders? No. But high-yielding stocks generally have lower growth prospects partly because they are paying out more of their profits in the form of dividends, thus leaving little to reinvest back into the company for growth.

What's also noteworthy about this is what I left out of the equation: dividend growth. On average, I expect a portfolio with a yield of 2 percent to have higher dividend growth than a portfolio with a 5 percent yield. In this case, though, I didn't even factor dividend growth into the mix. Had I done so, Portfolio B's returns would have been even more impressive.

It's about Time

How the cash flow is generated is only one piece of the puzzle.

When the cash flow is paid is also important. Even though you may not be taking home a paycheck, you still will have regular financial obligations, such as electric bills, credit-card bills, and mortgage or rent expenses. Most of your financial obligations will probably need to be addressed on a monthly basis.

From a budgeting standpoint, it is always nice to match up expenses with cash flows, which is why fixed-income investments (like money markets) are appealing. Comparatively, stock dividends are paid typically every three months (for U.S. stocks) or six months (for many international stocks).

How do you know when a company pays its dividend? The easiest way is to visit the company's web site and click on the "Investors Relations" link. Dividend information, including payment dates, can be found here. Alternatively, simply Google the company name along with the phrase "quarterly dividend payment." The results page should include a story about a recent dividend payment that will contain the payment date. If you don't have Internet access, call the company and ask for shareholder relations.

Making Sure You Have Dividends Every Month

Just because stocks pay dividends quarterly or semi-annually doesn't mean an investor can't receive dividend checks every month of the year to meet those financial obligations. All it takes is a little planning.

Medtronic is a leader in medical-technology equipment. The company has a strong position in cardiology and cardiovascular equipment. While the stock doesn't have a huge yield at 2 percent, Medtronic's dividend growth has been impressive. The company has boosted the payout every year since it was initiated in 1977. Furthermore, the pace at which the dividend has increased has been impressive—an average annual rate of roughly 20 percent over the last five years. Medtronic pays out that fast-rising dividend to its shareholders every January, April, July, and October.

Bristol-Myers Squibb is a stock I've owned for several years. Admittedly, there have been some rough patches with these shares. However, the company has made great strides in improving its operating picture, selling off slow-growth divisions while moving more aggressively into faster-growth biopharmaceuticals. One reason I like Bristol-Myers Squibb is its dividend yield of nearly 5 percent. While I reinvest my dividends to buy more Bristol-Myers stock (I talk about the power of dividend

LIFEGUARD ON DUTY [103]

reinvestment in Chapter 9), shareholders who take the cash receive a dividend check every February, May, August, and November.

When investors think of dividend stocks, Microsoft probably is not at the top of the list. However, given the prodigious cash flows the firm generates, the company should boost its dividend at a rate well above that of the average stock. Microsoft currently sends its quarterly dividend checks to shareholders in the months of March, June, September, and December.

Medtronic, Bristol-Myers Squibb, and Microsoft pay their dividends in different months. By owning one of the stocks, you would receive a dividend check four times a year. But if you viewed Medtronic, Bristol-Myers Squibb, and Microsoft as a "mini" three-stock portfolio, what you would discover is the following—by owning all three stocks, an investor would receive a dividend check every month of the year.

If predictable monthly cash flow is your aim, considering a company's dividend-payment schedule makes sense. I'm not suggesting that an investor own a lousy stock simply because it pays a dividend on a certain date. However, I am saying that knowing when dividends are paid, and perhaps tweaking a portfolio's composition to best meet recurring expenses, has its rewards. Perhaps the biggest benefit is a psychic one. Knowing you have cash flows matched up with expenses should take a lot of the uneasiness out of knowing whether you'll have enough money to pay the electric bill this month.

—————————————— ∼ ——————————————

By owning stocks with different dividend-payment dates, you can receive a dividend check every month of the year.

For assistance in constructing "dividends-every-month" portfolios, visit our web site www.bigsafedividends.com. Dividend-payment schedules for all stocks in the S&P 1500 Index are provided for free.

Yield!

- *Lifeguard on duty*. When draining the pool, start with an initial withdrawal rate of 3 to 4 percent.
- *Sell for cash*. Maximize the *total return* of your portfolio, regardless if you need cash flow from your investments. You can always sell stock to generate additional cash.
- *Stay in sync*. Sync cash flows with bills by matching dividend-payment schedules with monthly expenses.

Chapter Eight

Juice Your Portfolio without Striking Out

Take Disciplined Risk to Maximize Returns

I'M 49 YEARS OLD. Most guys my age hit golf balls for fun. I hit baseballs.

I love hitting baseballs so much I have my own batting cage, complete with a pitching machine I got through a buddy of mine who works for the Chicago White Sox. My pitching machine pumps fastballs up to 88 miles an hour, as well as curveballs, sliders, even drop balls.

I also hit baseballs thrown by humans. I play in a local Over-the-Hill league where all of the players in the league are 33 and older. I'm one of the older guys on my team, the Tigers. The oldest guy on the team is a 56-year-old recently retired steel worker, with a rubber arm and a bum hip.

The Tigers are, in a word, bad. We've won two games in two years (we've lost more than 30). I'd love to say it's not my fault.

I'd be lying.

Truth be told, I'm a pretty good hitter (after all, I do own my own batting cage). My fielding, on the other hand, is increasingly suspect. I'm finding it more difficult as the years go by to see fly balls (I play the outfield), especially during night games.

How could my team improve? We could get some younger guys on the team. We could practice more. We could take performance-enhancing drugs.

I sound absurd, suggesting that guys in their thirties, forties, and fifties would take steroids or human growth hormone (HGH) to perform better in an adult recreational baseball league. Actually, I wouldn't be shocked if there were guys in the league who juiced.

Why would anyone risk his or her health by taking performance-enhancing drugs? To get an edge on the competition, to maximize a finite talent.

For me, it makes no sense to use performance-enhancing drugs. But I can't make that call for others. For some people, the tradeoff of possible health effects is worth the extra bat speed or arm strength.

Another idea to consider is that, in some corners, taking anabolic steroids and human growth hormone is a perfectly legitimate form of therapy. Of course, it's one thing to self-medicate with performance-enhancing drugs; it's another to take them under the direction of a physician. Still, it can't be denied that, under certain circumstances and with proper direction, using these drugs can be beneficial.

What does all of this have to do with investing? Actually, the analogy of performance-enhancing drugs is an apt one in the context of dividend investing. Certain performance-enhancing dividend plays have the ability to turbo-charge your portfolio's yield. But these investments come with risks. This chapter examines a number of dividend-plays-on-steroids and discusses ways to use these investments in a prudent fashion.

The REIT Stuff

Real Estate investment trusts (REITs) are securities that trade like stocks. There are two main types of REITs. *Equity* REITs invest in and own properties (anything from strip malls to office buildings, industrial facilities to

health-care facilities), with revenue coming mostly from
rent. *Mortgage* REITs hold mortgages, generating revenue from interest on the loans. Both typically have high
yields, since they must distribute at least 90 percent of
their income to investors.

I know REITs have traditionally paid big dividends
and that in some years they have performed quite well,
but I've never been a big fan.

- Most REIT dividends don't receive the preferential
  15 percent tax rate afforded to other dividend-paying
  stocks. REIT cash flows are typically taxed at an
  individual's ordinary income tax rate, and REITs
  are dependent on the commercial and industrial
  real estate markets, which can be volatile. Currently
  many real estate markets, especially commercial real
  estate, are still limping along.
- REITs have extremely high payout ratios, which
  leaves them vulnerable to dividend cuts or omissions
  if problems occur.
- Most individuals already have a big bet on real
  estate via home ownership. Owning a bunch of REITs
  increases that exposure.

In recent years REIT dividends have become an
endangered species. According to data compiled by BMO

Capital Markets, at least 30 percent of all listed REITs have either cut or omitted their dividends or switched to paying the dividends in company stock within the last 18 months. Spurring the move to pay stock instead of cash was an Internal Revenue Service ruling that gave REITs the flexibility to pay as much as 90 percent of the intended dividend in the form of stock and just 10 percent in cash.

While this may sound like a good deal—and very much in the spirit of this book—it's not. In a dividend reinvestment plan, *you* decide whether you want to take your dividends in cash or reinvest them to buy additional shares; the company does not dictate the reinvestment for you. Not every shareholder chooses to reinvest dividends to buy additional shares. Those shareholders who reinvest dividends are increasing their percentage ownership in the company.

That is not what happened with these REIT stock dividends. Basically, the REIT is making the determination of how much in cash and how much in stock shareholders will receive. If virtually all shareholders receive the same percentage amount of stock, there is no percentage increase in their individual ownership; there are just more shares outstanding. In short, this is a stock split masquerading as a dividend; shareholders receive more shares, but their total percentage ownership doesn't change.

To make matters worse, under the IRS rule, REIT shareholders were taxed on the dividends received in stock, which is akin to paying taxes on a stock split.

Adding insult to injury, the fact that many REITs paid a large chunk of their dividends in the form of stock was not readily obvious when looking at a REIT's quoted yield.

The special ruling allowing REITs to pay dividends in stock applied to tax years ending on or before December 31, 2009. At the time of this writing, it was not determined whether the rules would be extended through 2010. To be on the safe side, make sure the REIT in which you are interested is paying its dividend with cash, not stock. You can confirm this by calling the company's shareholder-services department.

—————— ∽ ——————

Make sure the REIT is paying its dividend with cash, not stock.

I think it makes sense to diversify REIT exposure via a REIT mutual fund or exchange-traded fund. One worthwhile REIT fund is the Vanguard REIT Index (VNQ) exchange-traded fund. Additional REIT investments are listed at the end of this chapter.

Master Mines

Master limited partnerships (MLPs) are publicly traded partnerships that typically invest in hard assets—real estate, commodities, or energy-related assets like coal mines or natural-gas pipelines and storage facilities. Because of its structure, an MLP does not pay income taxes. Rather, income, depreciation, and expenses are "passed through" to partners (i.e., unit holders) based on their ownership stakes. The unit holders, in turn, are responsible for their own tax reporting. Similar to REITs, MLPs distribute the bulk of their cash flows to partners. Thus, yields tend to run well above those of common stocks.

As is the case with high-yielding REITs, high-yielding MLPs are not a free lunch:

- *MLPs are particularly sensitive to market volatility.* It doesn't do you much good if an investment yields 10 percent but declines 40 percent. That was the case for many MLPs in 2008. True, the group rebounded sharply in 2009. Still, investors should not ignore the potential volatility.

- *MLPs are also sensitive to interest rates.* Because of their high income streams, MLPs can behave similarly to fixed-income investments, falling in value when interest rates rise.

- *They rely on credit.* Many MLPs in capital-intensive sectors, such as energy distribution and storage, must access credit markets to fund expansion. If that access is impinged—as happened during the 2008 credit-market meltdown—MLPs could suffer.

- *They're especially susceptible to economic downturns.* One of the appeals of certain energy MLPs, especially those involved in natural-gas distribution and storage, is that their cash flows are not especially sensitive to energy prices. In fact, low natural-gas prices can sometimes spark greater demand for distribution and storage. However, economic weakness affects end-user demand for energy products, which impacts MLP volume and revenue regardless of commodity prices. That could lead to lower dividends.

- *They create potentially complex tax issues.* Investors in MLPs are limited partners. MLPs report tax information to limited partners via annual K-1 statements. If any of you have ever received a K-1, you know these are not the easiest documents to decipher come tax time. Adding to the complexity, some MLP investors may have to pay taxes in the various states where the partnership operates.

While MLPs may have a place in a yield-hungry investor's portfolio, exposure should be limited to 5 percent to

10 percent of a dividend portfolio. MLP recommendations are provided in the list at the end of this chapter.

Annuitize Me

One exotic income investment that is gaining investor interest is annuities. According to the insurance-industry group Limra International, the annuity market has grown by at least 50 percent in the past decade. Much of that growth reflects demographics. Aging investors want to reduce portfolio volatility, preserve wealth, and boost cash flow. Annuity sales pitches aim squarely at those three objectives.

But do annuities make sense for most investors? The question has no simple answer. The term "annuity" covers a wide array of investment vehicles.

The most straightforward of annuities is the immediate annuity.

Immediate annuities work like this: In return for a single payment to the annuity provider (usually an insurance company), an individual receives a fixed, guaranteed monthly cash flow for life.

With traditional immediate annuities, payments stop at death of the annuity holder. And the initial investment stays with the annuity seller. For example, if you buy an immediate annuity today and die tomorrow, your heirs typically will not receive any payments.

The amount of an immediate annuity's monthly cash flows is influenced by the size of the investment, age, and interest rates. According to ImmediateAnnuities.com, if a 65-year-old man purchases an immediate annuity for $200,000, he should expect to receive guaranteed monthly income of around $1,300 for the rest of his life. If he ponies up $500,000, the guaranteed monthly cash flow jumps to approximately $3,200. The cash flow is not affected by stock market ups and downs. It's not influenced by interest-rate movements. It is fixed for the life of the annuity owner.

The cash flows for this annuity reflect an annual distribution of nearly 8 percent of the original investment. How can the insurance company pay such a high distribution rate?

Because insurance companies pool funds from many annuity holders—and because payments to annuity holders are life-contingent—a portion of the assets contributed by those who die early finance higher payments to those who live longer. This allows annuity sellers to pay interest rates higher than the risk-free rate of a Treasury security.

Part of the monthly payment represents a return of investment. Since return of investment is not taxable, annuity owners pay taxes on only part of the cash flow. This is known as the "exclusion rate," which changes based on the investor's age.

In light of the market debacle of 2008 and the historically high rate of dividend cuts in the last 18 months, it's easy to see why investors are showing more interest in immediate annuities. For investors who desire more certainty and less volatility, immediate annuities make sense for at least part of their retirement investments.

But some features of immediate annuities may reduce their appeal:

- *Lack of flow-through to heirs can be a major turn-off.* Some immediate annuities will make ongoing payments to beneficiaries, but the annuity buyer must be willing to accept lower monthly cash payments.
- *Loss of control and access to the money.* If you need funds to meet a sudden financial obligation, the annuity does not offer liquidity.
- *Large opportunity costs.* While the fixed payments of immediate annuities look good in light of the market's decline in 2008, a holder of an immediate annuity did not benefit from the strong market rally in 2009.
- *Not all guarantees are created equal.* Annuity cash flows are guaranteed by the insurance company writing the annuity contract, not the government. The guarantee is only as good as the survivability of the insurer.

Should an insurance company become insolvent, State Guaranty Funds are set up to help protect annuity holders. However, there are many issues that can influence the extent of coverage. For further information about state guaranty funds, contact the National Organization of Life and Health Insurance Guaranty Associations (www .nolhga.com).

If you are still interested in annuities, check out the health of annuity companies by comparing ratings from the four independent rating agencies—Standard & Poor's, Moody's, A.M. Best, and Fitch. You should also consider diversifying annuity investments across multiple providers.

Because interest rates influence the size of annuity cash flows—and current rates are very low—it may make sense to spread out or "ladder" your purchases over time.

The top seller of immediate annuities is New York Life. In addition to insurance companies, most major brokerage firms and many mutual-fund families sell immediate annuities to investors, although an insurance company usually backs the annuity. To check out different immediate annuities, visit ImmediateAnnuities.com.

King Me

Like MLPs and REITs, the regal-sounding Royalty Trust is a "pass-through" investment. This means that these investments don't pay taxes at the corporate level; rather, income is "passed through" to investors, who pay the taxes. The trusts, which trade like stocks, are oftentimes involved in the energy and mining markets. These investments provide a direct way to invest in commodities.

There is a hitch, however. Royalty trusts have a finite life; they own royalties on resources that deplete over time. As the resources are eventually exhausted, so too are the royalties associated with those resources, hampering the trusts' ability to pay dividends.

A few of the more attractive royalty trusts are listed at the end of this chapter.

Preferred Seating

Preferred stocks are a little like common stocks and a lot like bonds. Preferred stockholders rank above common shareholders but below bond holders when it comes to getting their money if a company goes belly-up. They also receive preferential treatment when it comes to dividends. Dividends are paid to preferred shareholders before they are paid to common shareholders. If a dividend is not paid on a preferred, it accumulates from year to year. And before a dividend is paid to common shareholders, the cumulative dividends must be paid to preferred shareholders.

As with the other exotic investments we're talking about here, preferreds have some shortcomings. A big one is that preferred dividends tend to be fixed, so they're not a great hedge against inflation. Also, preferreds don't typically have the appreciation potential of common stocks. Finally, because preferreds derive the bulk of their return from income they tend to be much more interest-rate-sensitive than common stocks.

If you intend to purchase preferreds, stick to those rated at least BBB by Standard & Poor's and Baa by Moody's. Also, while most traditional preferred stocks pay dividends that qualify for the maximum 15 percent tax rate, there are many preferred-like-sounding investments that are really bonds in disguise and do not receive favorable tax treatment. A good source for information on preferreds, including their tax status, is quantumonline.com.

Favorite preferred stocks and preferred mutual funds are in the list at the end of this chapter.

Fund Time

Mutual funds are investments that pool money from a bunch of investors to buy a basket of stocks that is professionally managed by a fund manager. The major benefit of mutual funds is that they allow investors to diversify their dollars across a broad number of investments.

The most common form of mutual fund is the "open-end" mutual fund, which continuously buy and redeem shares for investors. These mutual funds do not trade on stock exchanges; rather, the prices of open-end mutual funds are set by the value of the underlying securities in the fund, also known as net asset value. Purchases and redemptions of open-end mutual funds are made at the end of each trading day. Popular open-end mutual fund families are Vanguard, T. Rowe Price, and Fidelity.

Open-end mutual funds differ from "closed-end" mutual funds, which *issue* a fixed number of shares at inception. Closed-end funds trade on an exchange throughout the day. The value of these shares is based on demand, meaning a closed-end fund's value can differ from the underlying value of securities in the portfolio. If a closed-end fund trades at a "discount," the underlying per-share value of the fund's securities is higher than the fund's per-share price. But, even at a discount, closed-end funds may not be good investments. Unrealized gains represent potential tax liabilities. Many closed-end funds use borrowed money (leverage) to provide higher yields and potentially higher returns. But leverage comes at a cost—decreased operating flexibility and increased share-price volatility.

The newest form of mutual fund is the exchange-traded fund (ETF). These funds resemble closed-end funds in that ETFs are bought and sold like stocks. The big difference with ETFs is their transparency. ETFs must disclose their holdings on a daily basis. That transparency has a lot of advantages for investors. For starters, you always know what you own with ETFs. That makes allocating investments easier in a portfolio. If you know a particular ETF has a big position in, say, IBM, it may not make sense to own IBM individually. Or if an ETF has a big exposure to a particular sector, say technology, it may influence how many technology stocks you own. The transparency differs from open-end mutual funds, which report their holdings only once a quarter.

Other advantages of exchange-traded funds include low expenses versus open-end mutual funds, trading flexibility (ETFs are bought and sold like stocks on the various exchanges), and tax efficiency, making them a solid choice for most investors.

When investing in mutual funds for dividends, make sure you understand the sector exposure of the fund. In 2008, many dividend mutual funds got hammered as a result of having too many financial stocks. For example, the iShares Dow Jones Select Dividend (DVY) exchange-traded fund fell approximately 33 percent primarily because of its big exposure to financials. Make sure that the dividend fund is properly diversified across a number of sectors.

Mutual funds—whether they are open-ends, closed-ends, or ETFs—are not inherently risky investments. The risk level depends on what the funds own. The good news for dividend investors is that there are many mutual funds from which to choose if you want to invest in dividend-paying stocks. The following list includes a variety of dividend-focused funds. All of the open-end mutual funds are "no-load" funds; that is, the funds can be bought directly from the fund company, without using a broker to conduct the transaction. Closed-end funds and ETFs are bought via brokers.

Make sure the dividend fund is properly diversified across a number of sectors.

Dividend Plays on Steroids

Royalty Trusts

BP Prudhoe Bay (BPT)

Cross Timbers (CRT)

Great Northern Iron Ore (GNI)

Mesa (MTR)

Sabine (SBR)

Master Limited Partnerships

Alliance Resource (ARLP)

Markwest Energy (MWE)

Penn Virginia Resource (PVR)

Suburban Propane (SPH)

Sunoco Logistics (SXL)

REITs

Brookfield Properties (BPO)

National Retail Properties (NNN)

Rayonier (RYN)

Ventas (VTR)

Preferred Stocks

Consolidated Edison N.Y. (ED-A)

Metlife (MET-B)

RenaissanceRe (RNR-D)

Vornado Realty Trust (VNO-I)

Open-End Funds

Fidelity Dividend Growth (FDGFX)

Royce Dividend Value (RYDVX)

Schwab Dividend Equity Select (SWDSX)

T. Rowe Price Dividend Growth (PRDGX)

Vanguard Dividend Growth (VDIGX)

Closed-End Funds

Eaton Vance Enhanced Equity Inc. (EOI)

Eaton Vance Tax Advantaged Div. Inc. (EVT)

Gabelli Dividend & Income (GDV)

Nuveen Equity Premium Opportunity (JSN)

Exchange-Traded Funds

Claymore/Zacks Dividend Rotation (IRO)

Dow Diamonds Trust (DIA)

First Trust Morningstar Dividend Leaders (FDL)

First Trust Value Line Dividend (FVD)

iShares Dow Jones Select Dividend (DVY)

iShares S&P U.S. Preferred Stock (PFF)

PowerShares Dividend Achievers (PFM)

PowerShares High Yield Divi. Achievers (PEY)

SPDR S&P 500 (SPY)

SPDR S&P Dividend (SDY)

SPDR S&P International Divi. (DWX)

Vanguard Dividend Appreciation (VIG)

Vanguard High Dividend Yield (VYM)

Vanguard REIT Index (VNQ)

WisdomTree Dividend Ex-Financials (DTN)

WisdomTree Equity Income (DHS)

WisdomTree LargeCap Dividend (DLN)

WisdomTree MidCap Dividend (DON)

WisdomTree SmallCap Dividend (DES)

WisdomTree Total Dividend (DTD)

Batter Up

A good hitter will tell you there's a very, very, *very* fine line between hitting a home run and striking out. What helps is knowing your strike zone and which pitches to swing at and which ones to lay off. Dividend investors have to know their strike zone, too—when to take their shot on a risky but high-yielding opportunity, and when to take a pass. This chapter discusses a number of high-risk but potentially high-reward investments that can help juice your portfolio's return. But like a hitter, don't over swing in your haste to hit one out of the park. Own these investments in moderation.

For ideas on mixing these investments in a portfolio, see our Ultimate Big, Safe Dividend Portfolio in Appendix B.

Yield!

- *Have a good eye at the plate*. Don't be swinging at every stock with a super-high yield. Be selective, focusing on those with good BSD and Quadrix scores. To obtain scores for REITs, MLPs, and royalty trusts, visit our web site—www.bigsafe dividends.com.

- *Expect to strike out a time or two*. Even the best baseball hitters are successful only 3 out of every 10 times at the plate. If you buy exotic dividend investments, be prepared to have some clunkers. For that reason, make sure your portfolio is not heavily weighted toward such risky investments. If you have more than 20 percent of a portfolio in the types of risky dividend stocks discussed in this chapter, that's too much.

- *Know the rule book*. REITs, MLPs, and royalty trusts typically do not receive favorable tax treatment; in most cases you will pay taxes on these investments at your ordinary tax rate. Make sure you take that into account when considering these investments versus dividend-paying stocks that qualify for the maximum 15 percent tax rate.

When DRIPs
Become Floods

~

Reinvest Your Way to Riches

I WROTE EARLIER IN THIS BOOK that had I been able to invest a relatively small amount of money in Exxon when I started working in 1982, I would be sitting on a pile of money today. Indeed, a $5,000 investment in Exxon in August 1982 is now worth $346,000. Dividends play a huge role in the growth of that investment. But you wouldn't have $346,000 worth of Exxon stock today if you cashed those quarterly dividend checks. The investment grew because those dividends were reinvested to buy more Exxon shares, and those new shares increased in value as a result of Exxon's price appreciation, and those new shares threw off additional dividends that were reinvested to buy still more shares that benefited from Exxon's price appreciation.

Dividend reinvestment is the essential component to building wealth with dividends. Notice I said *building wealth*, not *generating income*. There's nothing wrong with cashing your dividend checks to pay bills and fund your expenses; for some, it's a given, and this book has talked at great length about the power of dividend stocks to generate regular cash flows.

But if you want to build wealth over time, cashing your dividends is not the way to go. *Reinvesting them is.* By reinvesting dividends, you take advantage of what Einstein reportedly called the eighth wonder of the world—compounding. It's using your dividends to buy more shares of stock—with those shares producing more dividends to buy more shares, and so on, and so forth.

How can investors exploit the compounding of dividends via reinvestment? Actually, it is quite easy to reinvest. And, in most cases, it won't cost you a penny.

~

If you want to build wealth over time, cashing your dividends is not the way to go. Reinvesting them is.

DRIP Tease

If you buy stocks through a broker, it's a good bet that your broker offers dividend reinvestment. If it is available, make sure that there are no fees to reinvest dividends. Also, make sure the broker will buy full and fractional shares with your dividends. You want the dividends working for you as quickly as possible; you don't want the broker to hold your dividends and reinvest only when there is enough to buy a full share of stock.

Another method of reinvestment is to participate in company-sponsored *dividend reinvestment plans* (DRIPs). These plans, discussed briefly in Chapter 5, allow shareholders to purchase stock directly from companies. Investors purchase stock with dividends that the company reinvests for them in additional shares. Most DRIPs also permit investors to make voluntary cash payments directly into the plans to purchase shares.

DRIPs have several attractions for individual investors:

- In most cases, companies charge little or no commissions for purchasing stocks through their DRIPs.
- If your investment isn't enough to purchase a whole share, the company will purchase a fractional share, and the fractional share is entitled to that fractional part of the dividend.

- A number of DRIPs, as you'll soon read, permit participants to purchase stock at a discount to prevailing market prices. These discounts are usually 2 to 5 percent. Most discounts apply only to shares purchased with reinvested dividends, but some firms also apply the discount to purchases made with voluntary cash investments.

Enrolling in DRIPs differs, depending on the type of plan. Traditional DRIPs require investors to own at least one share of stock—and that share must be registered in the name of the shareholder, not the broker—in order to join the plan. The one-share requirement does make it more difficult to get started investing directly. Fortunately, as discussed in Chapter 5, many companies have taken their DRIPs to the next level by allowing any investor to buy stock directly, the first share and every share.

Approximately 1,100 U.S. and international companies offer DRIPs. Investors literally have the world at their fingertips when it comes to reinvesting dividends.

Everyone Wins

Obviously, the benefits of DRIPs for an individual investor are many. But what does a company get out of offering a plan?

One company benefit is improved shareholder relations. Companies believe DRIPs build goodwill with shareholders—goodwill that can translate into a number of benefits. For example, many retailers and consumer-products companies offer DRIPs. These companies understand the synergy that operates between shareholder and customer. A shareholder is more likely to buy the goods and services of a company in which it owns stock than the goods and services of a company in which it is not a shareholder.

Another benefit a company may derive from its DRIP is a more diverse and stable shareholder base. Many corporations and management are under the gun from shareholder activists who demand to have their voices heard concerning the operations of these companies. Individual investors tend to be more loyal than institutional investors, and they are generally less vocal, which is one reason companies like to have a good representation of individual investors in their shareholder mix. Widely dispersed ownership of stock also makes it more difficult for companies or investment groups to acquire large blocks that could be used in a takeover battle.

Perhaps the most compelling reason a company would offer a DRIP is that the plans are an effective way to raise cash. Many companies issue new shares in their DRIPs, thereby raising equity capital in a way that is similar to floating stock via an investment banker.

Carrot on a Stick

One way a company can draw investor funds to raise equity capital is by giving DRIP participants a discount on shares purchased through the plan. This discount—which is usually 2 percent to 5 percent of the market price—serves as a carrot to draw investors to the plan. From an investor perspective, buying stock at 95 cents on the dollar has its appeal. The 5 percent discount represents a downside cushion for investors. Also, by reinvesting dividends at a discount, you actually boost the effective dividend yield of your investment.

Let's say XYZ Corp. trades at $50 per share. It currently pays an indicated annual dividend of $2.25 per share, giving these shares a yield of 4.5 percent. This particular company offers a 5 percent discount on shares purchased with reinvested dividends via its DRIP, so if you reinvest those dividends to buy more shares, your purchase price with those dividends isn't $50 per share, but $47.50 per share (95 percent of $50 to reflect the 5 percent discount). Thus, your $2.25 dividend now yields more than 4.7 percent ($2.25 divided by $47.50).

You've just boosted your effective yield from 4.5 percent to 4.7 percent. That may not sound like much, but it actually is the equivalent of the company increasing its dividend approximately 5 percent. And 5 percent dividend growers have not exactly been prevalent lately.

Keep in mind, however, that you will get this yield-boosting discount only if you reinvest the stock via the company's DRIP. You will not likely receive the discount if you reinvest dividends via your broker's DRIP. The reason is that the broker's DRIP and the company's DRIP are two different plans. You can only enroll in the company plan if you are the registered shareholder. This is so important I'm going to repeat it—*you can only enroll in a company's sponsored DRIP if you are the registered shareholder*. If your shares are held at the broker, you are eliminated from participating in the company's DRIP.

I don't mean to bad-mouth broker reinvestment plans. In fact, most broker dividend reinvestment programs allow you to reinvest dividends on virtually any company that pays a dividend, including those that may not offer their own DRIP directly to investors. However, if you want to participate in DRIPs with discounts, you'll have to enroll directly in the company-sponsored plans.

Turning the Spigot On and Off

Companies usually give themselves the flexibility of implementing or curtailing discounts at a moment's notice, so it is not unusual for a company to offer a discount on voluntary cash investments one month and not the next. It is also not unusual for a company to alter the size of the discount. For example, a firm may implement a discount of 2 percent one month, jump it up to 4 percent the next month, and discontinue the discount the third month.

What drives company's discount policies is the need for cash. If a company doesn't need to raise money, it's not likely to offer a discount. If the firm has a project or investment that needs funding, a discount is more likely.

Not surprisingly, companies that consume lots of equity capital to run their businesses are the most likely providers of discounts. For example, real estate investment trusts, which require a constant stream of cash flow to fund their real estate endeavors, are a popular hunting ground for DRIP discounts. Other sectors where you see DRIP discounts include banks, utilities, and emerging companies.

If you are interested in investing in DRIPs that offer discounts, be aware of the following:

- Some companies offer discounts only on shares purchased with reinvested dividends. Others may apply the discount only to shares purchased with optional cash investments. Still others may apply the discount to both reinvested dividends and optional investments. It's important to read the DRIP prospectus to understand all of the details of the discount feature.

- Companies will offer discounts only on shares purchased from the company, not on shares the company purchases for DRIP participants on the open market.

- For those DRIPs that permit initial purchase directly, it is possible that the discount will not be applied to the initial purchase.
- Many DRIPs with discounts have "waiver" options. For example, if the maximum investment permitted in the DRIP is $5,000 per month, under certain circumstances, a company may waive that limit and allow individuals to invest larger amounts of money to receive the discount. Companies with waiver policies usually have phone numbers that investors can call to check whether a waiver is in place for that investment period. Waiver policies and the contact phone number are provided in the plan prospectus.
- Some companies may offer the discount only on investments in excess of a certain amount, usually $10,000.
- Be sure you understand how the discounted price is determined. Most companies have a "threshold pricing period" that establishes the stock price from which the discount will be given. It is not uncommon for a company to use the average trading price over a 5- or 10-day trading period as the baseline price from which the discount will be taken.

DRIP discount policies differ between companies, and the handling of the discount in some cases can be rather complicated in its execution. It is very important that investors read the plan prospectus so there are no surprises concerning the plan's discount terms and conditions. Most prospectuses are available online at the company's web site or the web site of the transfer agent administering the plan. A good starting point for information is the Investor Relations section of the company's web site.

Of course, just because a DRIP offers a discount does not make it a great investment. The company may be offering the discount because it is desperate for cash. It's important to do your homework when choosing DRIPs with discounts. One company worth mentioning is Aqua America (WTR), the leading water utility in the United States. Aqua America offers a 5 percent discount on reinvested dividends. Aqua America has a very user-friendly DRIP. You can make even your initial investment directly with the company. Minimum initial investment is $500. There are no purchase fees in the plan. The DRIP also has an IRA option whereby participants can invest directly with Aqua America and have those investments go into a traditional or Roth IRA. For a prospectus and enrollment information, call the company's transfer agent, Computershare, at (800) 205-8314 or visit Computershare online at www.computershare.com.

A Sure Thing

I'm sure savvy readers have quickly seized on the following opportunity: If you buy stock at a discount via a DRIP, and simultaneously sell the same stock at the full market price, you pocket the discount. If you do that a dozen times a year, that's a pretty nice "guaranteed" return. A sure thing.

Actually, this is exactly what some professional investors try to do with DRIP discounts. It's called "arbitrage." Put simply, arbitrage is the practice of taking advantage of price discrepancies in different markets for the same product.

Here's an example of a shopping arbitrage that actually happened to a friend of mine. (I may be a little off on the exact numbers here, but you'll get the gist of it.) This friend bought a dress (I believe at Neiman Marcus) for 50 percent of its $300 price tag, or $150. About a week later, she was shopping at a different Neiman Marcus and saw the same dress for $300. What she decided to do was a little dress "arbitrage." She took the dress back to the second Neiman Marcus and received $300. She then returned to the first Neiman Marcus, where the dress was still on sale for $150, and bought the dress.

This "arbitrage" basically netted my friend a free dress. Let's run through the math again:

1. She spent $150 for the original dress (out $150, but has a dress).

2. She received $300 when she returned the dress to the second store. (She is now up $150, but without a dress.)

3. She returned to the first store where the dress was on sale and bought the dress back for $150 (free dress).

Setting aside the ethics of the situation for a moment, the fact that the same dress was selling at two different prices provided an opportunity for profit. This is essentially what professional investors do with DRIP discounts:

1. Enroll in a DRIP that offers a discount.
2. Purchase the maximum amount of stock permitted.
3. Immediately sell the stock (in many cases, via a "short sale") in the open market to capture the price differential.

Such activity presents a quandary for companies. On the one hand, companies like discounts because they enhance the DRIP's ability to raise money. On the other hand, such arbitrage activity can heighten the stock's volatility. Furthermore, some companies resent the fact that arbitrage activity is being conducted by professional investors when their plans are intended primarily for small investors. For that reason, most companies reserve the right to terminate a DRIP account if the firm believes the account is being used to arbitrage the discount.

If you plan to attempt this type of arbitrage—and I don't recommend this for most investors, given the complexity of the task—keep in mind the following:

- *The arbitrage is best done using DRIPs that offer discounts on optional cash investments.* The profit potential from arbitraging the discount on reinvested dividends is limited unless you hold many shares.

- *Consider the amount of Optional Cash Payments permitted and how often OCPs are invested.* The larger the maximum amount of Optional Cash Payments permitted in the plan, and the more frequent investors can make those OCPs, the larger the potential profit. Several plans have "waiver" options whereby firms, depending on their need for capital, will give permission to investors to invest amounts greater than the maximum investments listed in the plan prospectus.

- *Consider the size of discount.* Obviously, profit potential is greater with a 5 percent discount than a 2 percent discount.

- *Look at pricing periods.* This is perhaps the most crucial point to consider, and the one that is making the discount arbitrage more difficult. Many companies with discounts have implemented multiday pricing periods—5 to 10 days and even longer in some cases—which are used to determine the purchase price in the DRIP. (Pricing periods are explained in company DRIP prospectuses.) What these pricing periods do is make it more difficult to determine at what price you'll be purchasing shares. If you know that the company buys stock on the last day of the month with Optional Cash Payments and the purchase price will be the average price on that day, then you know at what price you must short the stock in the market in order to lock up a profit. However, when a company uses a pricing period to compute the price—for example, the purchase price is the average of the high and low price per day over a 10-day period—it makes it more difficult to determine your purchase price. Also, such pricing periods may distort the size of the discount. For example, let's say a stock's average price during the 10-day pricing period is $10. However, on the close of the tenth day, the stock is trading for $9. The discount (let's say 5 percent) is applied to the average price over the 10-day period ($10), giving DRIP participants a purchase price of $9.50 ($10 multiplied by 0.95). However, in this scenario, you'd be better off buying the stock at the market price since it is cheaper than the "discounted" price. Conversely, it is possible that a 5 percent discount can expand to 10 percent or more if the stock jumps sharply at the end of a pricing period. Understanding how the pricing period works is critical to a successful arbitrage.

- *Consider the trading volume of the stock.* If you plan to short the stock in the market in order to lock up your profit, make sure the daily trading volume of the stock is sufficient to support short selling. In some cases, it may be difficult to execute the short sale if the stock is thinly traded.
- *Commissions matter.* Keep in mind that the commission you pay to sell the stock on the open market reduces your profit spread. Make sure you are not paying too much in commissions.

Again, if you are considering arbitraging DRIP discounts, it is imperative that you read closely the DRIP prospectus, which explains such important issues as threshold pricing periods, discount eligibility, waiver options, and so on.

The Best of Both Worlds

If you require cash dividends to meet your income needs, you may be disheartened after reading this chapter. Dividend reinvestment affords tremendous wealth-creation opportunities, and investors who reinvest dividends in certain companies get a better deal in terms of discounts than those who receive the dividends in cash.

What if you could have your cake and eat it, too? What if you could reinvest part of your dividends to buy additional shares while receiving the remainder in cash to meet your expenses?

Actually, you can. It's called partial reinvestment.

With the partial reinvestment option, investors can select the percentage of dividends they want to receive in cash and the percentage they want to reinvest to buy additional shares.

Partial reinvestment is offered by most company-sponsored DRIPs. To participate in partial reinvestment, just check the appropriate box on the DRIP enrollment form and provide instructions on the percentage of dividends you want to reinvest and the percentage you want to receive in cash.

Keep Those Statements

If you do reinvest dividends, whether via a broker or a company-sponsored DRIP, it's imperative that you maintain good records. Reinvesting relatively small amounts of money to buy fractional shares does pose some challenges when you sell your stock and have to determine your cost for tax purposes. If you have your statements, you will ease this burden significantly.

Uncle Sam Still Gets His

Some of you may think that dividend reinvestment provides the perfect tax loophole. "If I take the cash dividend, I have to pay taxes. But if I reinvest the dividend, I never receive the cash and therefore won't have to pay taxes on the dividends."

Wrong!

Just because you reinvest dividends doesn't mean you can avoid paying Uncle Sam taxes on those dividends. You'll pay taxes whether you receive cash dividends or reinvest them. In addition, if you reinvest dividends at a discount, the dollar value of the discount will more than likely be reported as taxable income. However, the IRS is somewhat ambiguous on the tax ramifications if you make optional cash investments in a DRIP and receive a discount. It's always a good idea to consult your tax advisor with questions concerning discounts on reinvested dividends and optional cash investments.

Say Good-Buy to Fear

I feel pretty confident saying that no one enjoys doing their taxes, but it does provide a helpful snapshot of financial behavior for the year. One of the things that struck me when doing my taxes was the amount of dividends I reinvested in 2008 via DRIPs. The thousands of dollars I reinvested to buy more shares probably did not produce much in the way of immediate profits; in fact, considering how ugly 2008 was, many of the shares I bought with those reinvested dividends are still probably showing losses. The interesting thing was that, because of my DRIPs, I had invested money during the worst stock market in more than 70 years.

And I was *happy* that I did.

I realize this sounds a bit . . . bonkers. Who would want to invest during such a terrible market?

Everyone.

It's always seemed illogical we tend to get most excited about buying stocks when they are expensive and most fearful of buying when they are on sale. If Apple had a half-off sale on iPods, iPhones, and Macs, consumers would stampede stores to take advantage of the discounts. But not the stock market. The Dow Jones Industrial Average fell roughly 50 percent from May 2008 to March 2009. How many of you were rushing to put more money into stocks? Nobody wants to buy a stock only to see it go down, but when you look at the fortunes created in the stock market, most involve individuals who are willing to buy during especially bleak market periods. As Warren Buffett likes to say, "Be greedy when others are fearful." The payoff usually isn't instant, and some pain (and a lot of second guessing) usually occurs. But buying quality stocks—companies with strong financial positions, industry-leading positions, and safe and steady dividend streams—during a bear market can be part of a winning recipe for long-term success in the market.

You probably know this already but are finding it tough to buy when markets are getting creamed. One of the most underrated aspects of dividend reinvestment is the "forced buying" that occurs with each dividend that is automatically reinvested to buy shares. In fact, reinvesting dividends may be the *only* way some of us buy during down markets. Dividend reinvestment takes the decision making out of your hands, and by doing so strips the investment process of emotion. That's a good thing. Emotions oftentimes make us do the wrong things. Dividend reinvestment is the closest thing to "emotionless" investing there is.

Reinvesting dividends may be the *only* way some of us buy during down markets.

Yield!

- *Take a pass on the cash.* If you are not dependent on dividends to meet your basic financial needs, plough those dividends back into the company to buy more shares.

- *Do it for free.* Don't pay fees to reinvest dividends. If your broker or DRIP charges a reinvestment fee, find another broker or DRIP.

- *Discount shopping.* Reinvesting dividends assures that you'll buy stocks when they go on sale.

Chapter Ten

If You Build It, Dividends Will Come

~

*Creating Your Own Yield
of Dreams*

THE INGREDIENTS OF A FLOURLESS CHOCOLATE CAKE, by themselves, are barely edible. Put them together and it's culinary magic.

Peyton Manning is nothing without Reggie Wayne and Dallas Clark to catch his passes and his offensive line to keep him upright.

Bonnie needed Clyde. Abbott needed Costello. Captain needed Tennille. Homer needed Marge.

Most investors focus on the parts—their individual stocks. The reality, however, is that long-term investment success depends on the whole—your portfolio. This chapter addresses key points to consider when building portfolios, concluding with a variety of big, safe dividend portfolios.

Long-term investment success depends on the whole—your portfolio.

Order This Free Lunch

Mention diversification and most investors' eyes glaze over. It's not riveting stuff. Besides, diversification doesn't work anymore, right? Just look at what happened to supposedly diversified portfolios in 2008.

While most asset classes were trashed in 2008, keep in mind that 2008 was the worst year in the stock market since 1931. So it's a bit unfair to use an outlier like 2008 as your litmus test for diversification. However, even if you do, 2008 doesn't refute the benefits of diversification.

Diversification is merely the grouping of investments with varying correlation of returns. And while it may not have felt like it, there was plenty of separation in returns between asset classes in 2008. Emerging market stocks plummeted 55 percent. Large-cap U.S. stocks fell around 37 percent. Junk bonds fell 26 percent. Short-term municipal bonds were flat. Long-term Treasuries were *up* around 9 percent. With large-cap U.S. stocks outperforming emerging market stocks by 18 percentage points, and long-term Treasuries outperforming large-cap U.S. stocks by *more than 45 percentage points*, arguing that diversification didn't matter in 2008 seems, well, silly.

The bottom line is that diversification worked in 2008, and it will work going forward. In fact, I would go as far as to say that diversification may be the only true free lunch in the stock market. By employing diversification correctly, investors can reduce portfolio risk without sacrificing returns. Notice I used the term "correctly." Lots of dividend investors thought they had diversified portfolios in 2008 because they owned lots of stocks. But those stocks clustered in only a few industries, such as financials and utilities. The market's gravitational pull affected all of the stocks equally. They were basically the same stock replicated 20 or 30 times over.

———————————— ∾ ————————————

By employing diversification *correctly*, investors can reduce risk without sacrificing returns.

Proper diversification has four important components:

1. *Diversification* across *assets*. Otherwise known as asset allocation, this form of diversification considers how much money to hold in stocks versus bonds and other asset classes. The goal, of course, is to own asset classes that are not closely correlated with one another. Yes, perhaps correlations are tightening between asset classes, especially on the equity side. Still, return spreads are significant enough to warrant spreading your bets across assets. Remember—while large-cap U.S. stocks fell 37 percent in 2008, long-term Treasuries rose 9 percent. Highly correlated asset classes? I don't think so.

2. *Diversification* within *assets*. This form of diversification spreads your bets within asset groups, such as within stocks (large, small, midsized, and international stocks) and bonds (short-term, long-term, government, corporate, and tax-exempt bonds).

3. *Diversification* across time. Investing on a regular basis spreads your bets across time. Dividend reinvestment is really a form of time diversification. By feeding money into the market on a regular basis, you avoid putting all of your funds in the market at the top.

4. *Diversification* across investment strategies. Portfolio diversification can be improved by including investment strategies that are not highly correlated. Diversifying across strategies is akin to the idea of "core and satellite" investing. For example, if you believe in passive investing, you may take the bulk of your investment dollars and invest in index funds covering a variety of asset classes. That's the "core" of your portfolio. But you want to diversify your primary strategy with other investment strategies. This "satellite" portion of your portfolio may focus on actively managed mutual funds or commodities.

When implementing these forms of diversification, you'll need to make decisions as to your proper portfolio mix between stocks and bonds, the appropriate dollar investment to put in each investment, the most suitable investment accounts (IRAs versus non-IRAs) to house certain portfolio investments, and the timing as to rebalancing your portfolio.

Stocks versus Bonds

How much should you have in stocks versus bonds? I hate to give a one-size-fits-all answer because everyone is different. But a useful starting point for determining your optimal asset allocation is to subtract your age from 110. Consider that percentage a benchmark for the percentage of equity in your portfolio. (Some financial planners use 100 instead of 110, but I think that leaves you with too little equity exposure in most cases.) Thus, a 50-year old could consider 60 percent equity as a good starting point. If the 50-year old has few financial responsibilities, a solid pension, many assets, and a high risk tolerance, equity exposure of 70 percent or even 80 percent may make sense. Conversely, some 50-year-olds may feel more comfortable with 40 percent or 50 percent equities.

A word of advice: While setting the appropriate asset allocation is a fairly personal decision, a common mistake investors make is to be too conservative. According to the U.S. Centers for Disease Control, the average 65-year-old can expect to live another 19 years. That length of time demands a healthy equity component in a portfolio to overcome the ravages of inflation.

The Weighting Game

Once you have made the proper asset-allocation choice, you'll need to construct "mini" portfolios that focus on the various asset classes (stocks, bonds, and so on). This section focuses on the stock portion of the portfolio.

How many stocks are enough? If you are incorporating large, midsize, and small stocks, you should probably hold 35 to 45 stocks. There was a time when I would have argued that 35 to 45 stocks were too many, but I've changed my tune a bit. It's tough to cover all of the necessary equity types with just 15 or 20 stocks. I think 35 to 45 stocks is small enough to still give your best investment ideas ample leverage yet large enough so that you don't have too much riding on a few stocks.

Once you've decided on the number of stocks, the next step is to weight the investments in your portfolio. One strategy is to weight your investments by market capitalization (outstanding shares multiplied by the share price). Stocks with the highest market cap would get the highest weighting in your portfolio. Most major market indexes are cap-weighted. Another option is to have approximately equal dollar amounts in each of your investments.

A word of advice: I believe that the best approach for most individual investors is to equal-weight or nearly equal-weight portfolios. In that way, you spread your bets and avoid the type of concentrated holdings that reduce portfolio diversification.

A Taxing Matter

Taxes matter when it comes to investing. Although too many investors make bad decisions in the name of reducing tax liabilities, prudent portfolio construction takes taxes into account.

For example, all things being equal, bonds and high-yielding stocks are best held in tax-preferenced accounts like IRAs. An exception to this rule would be if you need the cash flow from your investments to pay expenses. In that case, you'll probably need to have your cash-flow-generating investments in a non-IRA account so that you have fewer restrictions on accessing the money. Also, investments in which you plan a high level of turnover—frequent buying and selling—are best held in IRAs. Alternatively, investments that you plan to hold for the long term make sense for non-IRA accounts.

A word of advice: When possible, shield your income-generating and high-turnover investments in IRAs and place your low-turnover or low-yielding investments in taxable accounts.

Balancing Act

Over time your optimal asset allocation may diverge as a result of price changes. Rebalancing brings your allocation back to your model.

For example, let's say your optimal asset allocation is 65 percent stocks and 35 percent bonds. Over time, your equity allocation has grown to 70 percent. Should you rebalance? Perhaps, but consider the costs of that rebalancing. You may end up paring back positions in attractive stocks. Also, rebalancing may increase your tax bill.

A few percentage points over a particular allocation may not necessarily mandate strict rebalancing. On the other hand, if your asset allocations are out of whack by 10 percent or more—or an individual stock accounts for more than 7 percent of your entire portfolio—you may have reason to rebalance.

A word of advice: Consider rebalancing in your most tax-friendly accounts first (such as IRAs) in order to bring overall allocations back into balance. Next, focus rebalancing on investments with losses or those with long-term gains.

Armed with these portfolio construction concepts, let's build a few big, safe dividend portfolios.

Utility Lover's Portfolio

I almost don't want to give this portfolio, as it goes against everything I've just written about portfolio construction. But I know that plenty of you reading this want to own the best utilities. If you are one of those investors, here's a utility portfolio to consider:

AGL Resources (AGL)

Aqua America (WTR)

Avista (AVA)

CenterPoint Energy (CNP)

Dominion Resources (D)

DPL (DPL)

Energen (EGN)

Exelon (EXC)

FirstEnergy (FE)

FPL Group (FPL)

ITC Holdings (ITC)

OGE Energy (OGE)

Oneok (OKE)

Public Service Enterprise (PEG)

Questar (STR)

Southern Union (SUG)

UGI (UGI)

My preference is that you use this portfolio as a piece of a broader income portfolio. With the exceptions of Exelon and ITC, the stocks offer direct-purchase plans whereby any investor may buy the first share and every share directly from the company.

Mutual Fund Lover's Portfolio

Stocks or funds? It doesn't have to be an either/or proposition. Owning stocks *and* funds works when constructing a dividend portfolio. Still, some investors want nothing to do with individual stocks. For them, the following is a portfolio of attractive dividend mutual funds and ETFs.

Exchange-Traded Funds

iShares S&P U.S. Preferred Stock (PFF)

SPDR S&P Dividend (SDY)

SPDR S&P International Dividend (DWX)

Vanguard Dividend Appreciation (VIG)

Vanguard High Dividend Yield (VYM)

Vanguard REIT (VNQ)

Open-End Mutual Funds

Royce Dividend Value (RYDVX)

Vanguard Dividend Growth (VDIGX)

Closed-End Fund

Eaton Vance Enhanced Equity Income (EOI)

Notice that this portfolio includes U.S. and foreign stocks, as well as some of the more exotic dividend investments discussed in Chapter 8. Investors may purchase open-end funds either directly from the fund families or via most brokerage firms. Closed-end funds and ETFs need to be purchased via a broker.

The Ultimate Big, Safe Dividend Portfolio

For investors who want a broad-based dividend portfolio, the Ultimate Big, Safe Dividend Portfolio should work nicely. The portfolio offers attractive current yield (the average yield of the portfolio, assuming equal dollar investments in each investment, is nearly 4 percent), ample dividend-growth potential, and above-average appreciation potential. The portfolio, which pays monthly income, encompasses a variety of dividend investments—stocks (large, midsized, and small), funds, master limited partnerships, REITs, and international investments. It is an easy portfolio to continue making regular investments via dividend reinvestment and optional investments.

The complete portfolio is shown in Appendix B.

Ready, Set, Go Online

One of the shortcomings of any investment book is that things can change between the time the book is written and when it is read. Of course, to not make specific recommendations as a result of this timing issue would be a disservice to readers. People want actionable advice. The stocks, funds, and portfolios discussed in this chapter and, indeed, throughout the book represent my best ideas at the time of this writing. And I am comfortable that these ideas will hold up over time. Still, things change. For my most up-to-date thinking on dividend stocks, including current BSD and Quadrix scores on all stocks in the S&P 1500 Index, visit our free web site, www.bigsafedividends.com.

Yield!

- *Age-old wisdom*. Subtract your age from 110, and that is a benchmark for determining the appropriate percentage of stock in your portfolio.

- *Avoid portfolio vertigo*. If your optimal allocation between stocks and bonds gets out of whack by 10 percent or more, it's time to rebalance your portfolio.

- *Weighty matters*. When creating a portfolio, investing equal dollars in each investment will help ensure your portfolio doesn't get overweighted in just a few stocks.

Appendix A

∼

Advanced BSD Formula

THE ADVANCED BSD FORMULA uses 10 factors to evaluate dividend stability and growth:

1. *Payout ratio.* You knew this would be included in the advanced formula. And it carries the greatest weighting at 30 percent of the total model. This metric can be obtained from company financials, *Value Line*, or Yahoo!Finance (finance.yahoo.com) (30 percent weighting).

2. *Interest coverage.* Companies with lots of debt may struggle to pay the dividend if business conditions deteriorate. A company can't get rid of interest

payments on its debt (unless it repays the debt or goes bust). A company can get rid of the dividend. Interest coverage measures how well the company's profits cover its interest payments. This metric can be obtained via company financial statements or *Value Line* (10 percent weighting).

3. *Cash flow to net income.* We've talked a lot about profits as being the primary funding source of dividends. And that's true, to a point. But profits that are profits only on paper—that is, profits that are a figment of accounting magic—won't pay the dividend. You need actual cash to pay the dividend. Cash flow is calculated by adding noncash charges (such as depreciation) to net income after taxes. Cash flow to net income shows the relationship of cash to profits. This metric can be found on a company's financial statements, *Value Line*, or Yahoo!Finance (5 percent weighting).

4. *Dividend yield.* I did include dividend yield in the Advanced BSD Formula, giving weight to stocks with higher yields. However, the weighting of this metric is only 5 percent of the total. A stock's dividend yield can be obtained online at a number of finance sites (such as Yahoo!Finance) or in *Barron's* each week (5 percent weighting).

5. *Six-month relative strength.* This metric measures the stock's relative price performance over the last

six months. You may wonder why I included a stock-performance metric in this formula. Stock price movements are anticipatory. Stocks tend to crater prior to dividend cuts or omissions. Admittedly, this metric is not easily found, but you can get a decent proxy for a stock's relative strength by looking at its 12-month price performance relative to the S&P 500 Index. You can find this comparison in the "Key Statistics" part of a stock's profile at Yahoo!Finance. Just enter the ticker and click the link to "Key Statistics" on the left-hand side of the page (10 percent weighting).

6. *Tangible change in one-year book value.* This metric is a mouthful but really is quite simple. A company's book value is a quick (albeit imperfect) proxy for a company's intrinsic value. A "tangible" change in book value provides a nice check on a company's balance-sheet quality. Is the book value increasing due to an increase in intangibles? (Intangibles are those touchy-feely things, like goodwill, that are truly hard to value accurately and could artificially inflate a company's book value.) Or is book value increasing because of growth in retained earnings and other measures relevant to dividend safety? This metric can be computed from company financial statements, which are available at most

company web sites or the SEC's web site (www
.sec.gov) (10 percent weighting).

7. *Long-term expected profit growth.* Obviously, the company's ability to increase the dividend over time
depends in large part on its ability to increase profits. This metric looks at expected profit growth over
the next five years, based on the earnings estimates
of Wall Street analysts who follow the company. Is
this a perfect measure? No. But it is a reasonable
way to get some reading on a firm's future profit
growth. *Value Line* provides its version of a long-
term expected profit growth. Yahoo!Finance also
provides a long-term expected profit growth rate
(10 percent weighting).

8. *Three-year cash-flow growth.* This is a backward-
looking metric to see how successful the company
has been in increasing cash flow. Of course, past is
not always prologue, which is why I only give this
metric a 5 percent weighting. Still, there is something to be said for companies that have a record
of boosting cash flows on a regular basis. You can
obtain this metric from the company's financial
statements or *Value Line* (5 percent weighting).

9. *Three-year dividend growth.* Just because a company
has boosted its dividend regularly doesn't mean it
will do so in the future. Still, companies that have

a bent toward raising their dividend on a regular basis will likely try to do so barring a catastrophe. This metric can be obtained from company financial statements or *Value Line* (10 percent weighting).

10. *Three-year earnings growth*. Another backward-looking metric that provides some idea of how successful the company has been in boosting earnings. Again, past performance is not necessarily indicative of future results. Still, I would much prefer betting on a company with a history of boosting earnings than one that does not (5 percent weighting).

The Advanced BDS Formula also includes the same Overall Quadrix overlay as the Basic Formula to spotlight stocks with the best total-return potential.

Behold the Power of the Formula

We used the advanced model to compute BSD scores for stocks in the S&P 1500 Index going back to 1994. Each stock's BSD score reflects the weighted composite score of all 10 factors in the model. We then looked at stocks with BSD scores in the top quintile (80 and higher). We filtered that group down to stocks with an Overall Quadrix score of at least 75.

The results were impressive:

- Had you created a portfolio at the beginning of each year of all of the stocks in the S&P 1500 Index that met the above criteria (BSD scores of 80 and higher, Overall Quadrix scores of 75 and higher), you would have outperformed the S&P 1500 Index by *more than six percentage points per year* going back to December 31, 1994. That performance was even better than our Basic BSD Formula.

- Not only were your returns much better than the S&P 1500 Index, but the Advanced BSD Formula achieved those superior returns at a *lower risk level* than the index as measured by standard deviation.

- Had you picked stocks at the beginning of 2008 using the Advanced BSD Formula (BSD scores of 80 and higher and Overall Quadrix of 75 and higher), the probability of owning a stock that cut or omitted its dividend was virtually nil. Indeed, only *two* stocks from the S&P 1500 Index meeting these criteria at the beginning of 2008 cut their dividends during the year. That was during one of the worst years ever for dividend cuts and omissions.

We did not back-test our way into this model. Our analysts sat down and considered those metrics we felt had the most bearing on dividends. We then constructed the model, *then* went back to see how it would have done.

The following is a sampling of dividend-paying stocks that meet the following criteria:

- Advanced BSD scores of 80 and above.
- Overall Quadrix scores of 75 and above.
- Yields of 2.5 percent or more.

	Dividend Yield (%)
Abbott Laboratories (ABT)	3.0
Alcon (ACL)	2.5
AstraZeneca (AZN)	4.6
Automatic Data Processing (ADP)	3.1
Biovail (BVF)	2.7
Brookfield Properties (BPO)	5.2
Buckle (BKE)	2.8
Darden Restaurants (DRI)	3.2
DCP Midstream Partners (DPM)	9.4
EV Energy Partners (EVEP)	11.9
Hawkins (HWKN)	2.6
Innophos Holdings (IPHS)	3.1
ITC (ITC)	2.8
Legacy Reserves (LGCY)	11.9
Linn Energy (LINE)	10.3
Meridian Bioscience (VIVO)	3.0
National Healthcare (NHC)	2.8
Olin (OLN)	4.8
Polaris Industries (PII)	3.4
Safety Insurance (SAFT)	4.5

(Continued)

	Dividend Yield (%)
Sanofi-Aventis (SNY)	3.0
Shaw Communications (SJR)	4.2
Sysco (SYY)	3.6
WD-40 (WDFC)	3.0

Please be aware that BSD and Quadrix scores, as well as dividends and yields, will change over time. For the most up-to-date BSD and Overall Quadrix scores, visit our web site: www.bigsafedividends.com.

Appendix B

~

The Ultimate Big, Safe Dividend Portfolio

Common Stocks	Estimated Dividend Yield (%)	Payment Schedule	Category
Abbott Laboratories (ABT)	3.0	Feb, May, Aug, Nov	Health Care
Aflac (AFL)*	2.6	Mar, Jun, Sep, Dec	Financials
Alcon (ACL)	2.5	Feb, May, Aug, Nov	Health Care
Aqua America (WTR)*	3.6	Mar, Jun, Sep, Dec	Utilities
AstraZeneca (AZN)*	4.6	Mar, Sep	Health Care
Automatic Data Processing (ADP)	3.1	Jan, Apr, Jul, Oct	Technology
Baxter Int'l (BAX)	2.1	Jan, Apr, Jul, Oct	Health Care
Buckle (BKE)	2.8	Jan, Apr, Jul, Oct	Consumer Discretionary
Chevron (CVX)*	3.5	Mar, Jun, Sep, Dec	Energy

(*Continued*)

Common Stocks	Estimated Dividend Yield (%)	Payment Schedule	Category
China Mobile (CHL)*	3.2	May, Aug	Telecom
Chubb (CB)	2.8	Jan, Apr, Jul, Oct	Financials
Clorox (CLX)*	3.3	Feb, May, Aug, Nov	Consumer Staples
Colgate-Palmolive (CL)*	2.1	Feb, May, Aug, Nov	Consumer Staples
Cracker Barrel (CBRL)*	2.3	Feb, May, Aug, Nov	Consumer Discretionary
Darden Restaurants (DRI)*	3.2	Feb, May, Aug, Nov	Consumer Discretionary
FPL (FPL)*	3.7	Mar, Jun, Sep, Dec	Utilities
General Dynamics (GD)	2.3	Feb, May, Aug, Nov	Industrials
Harris (HRS)	2.0	Mar, Jun, Sep, Dec	Technology
Hasbro (HAS)	2.7	Feb, May, Aug, Nov	Consumer Discretionary
Hormel Foods (HRL)	2.0	Feb, May, Aug, Nov	Consumer Staples
ITC (ITC)	2.8	Mar, Jun, Sep, Dec	Utilities
Johnson & Johnson (JNJ)	3.1	Mar, Jun, Sep, Dec	Health Care
McDonald's (MCD)*	3.5	Mar, Jun, Sep, Dec	Consumer Discretionary
Medtronic (MDT)*	2.0	Jan, Apr, Jul, Oct	Health Care
Microsoft (MSFT)*	1.8	Mar, Jun, Sep, Dec	Technology
Novartis (NVS)*	2.7	Feb	Health Care
Novo Nordisk (NVO)*	1.2	Mar	Health Care
Paychex (PAYX)*	4.0	Feb, May, Aug, Nov	Technology
PepsiCo (PEP)*	2.9	Mar, Jun, Sep, Dec	Consumer Staples
Sanofi-Aventis (SNY)*	3.0	May	Health Care
Sysco (SYY)	3.6	Jan, Apr, Jul, Oct	Consumer Staples
Travelers (TRV)	2.5	Mar, Jun, Sep, Dec	Financials

Common Stocks	Estimated Dividend Yield (%)	Payment Schedule	Category
UGI (UGI)*	3.4	Jan, Apr, Jul, Oct	Utilities
United Technologies (UTX)*	2.3	Mar, Jun, Sep, Dec	Industrials
Wal-Mart (WMT)*	2.0	Mar, Jun, Sep, Dec	Consumer Staples
Royalty Trusts			
BP Prudhoe Bay (BPT)	8.8	Jan, Apr, Jul, Oct	Energy
Real Estate Inv. Trusts			
Brookfield Properties (BPO)	4.9	Mar, Jun, Sep, Dec	Financials
National Retail Properties (NNN)*	7.7	Feb, May, Aug, Nov	Financials
Preferred Stocks			
Metlife (MET-B)	7.2	Mar, Jun, Sep, Dec	Financials
RenaissanceRe (RNR-D)	7.9	Mar, Jun, Sep, Dec	Financials
Limited Partnerships			
Alliance Resource (ARLP)	7.7	Feb, May, Aug, Nov	Energy
Sunoco Logistics (SXL)	7.1	Feb, May, Aug, Nov	Energy
Closed-End Funds			
Eaton Vance Enhanced Equity Inc. (EOI)	12.1	Monthly	Large-Cap Growth
Exchange-Traded Funds			
SPDR S&P Dividend (SDY)	3.7	Jan, Apr, Jul, Oct	Large-Cap Value
Vanguard Dividend Appreciation (VIG)	2.0	Mar, Jun, Sep, Dec	Large-Cap Blend
Vanguard High Dividend Yield (VYM)	3.1	Mar, Jun, Sep, Dec	Large-Cap Value

(*Continued*)

Common Stocks	Estimated Dividend Yield (%)	Payment Schedule	Category
Open-End Funds			
Royce Dividend Value (RYDVX)	1.2	Mar, Jun, Sep, Dec	Small-Cap Value
Vanguard Dividend Growth (VDIGX)	2.2	Jun, Dec	Large-Cap Value
Portfolio Yield	**3.6**		

*Offers a direct purchase plan.

Acknowledgments

~

IT TAKES A VILLAGE to write a book.

It starts with a great agent, and I've got one in Wes Neff. Thanks, Wes, for encouraging me to get back in the game.

It takes a great support crew. Mine includes two brainiacs, David Wright and Jerome Kolacinski. These guys crunched a lot of numbers for me, and for that I am very grateful. I'd also like to thank the rest of my colleagues at Horizon Investment/Horizon Publishing, especially Rich Moroney, Bob Sweet, and Shelby Cavanaugh, for their ideas and support.

It takes top-notch editors to pull it all together. Special thanks go to Pamela van Giessen and Emilie Herman at John Wiley & Sons for their patience and guidance.

Finally, it takes great family and friends to put up with you during the process. I'd like to thank my parents, Bud and Frances Carlson, who have been with me in spirit every step of the way. Special thanks also goes to Denise, the love of my life, for giving me time off from yard work to write. I'd also like to acknowledge R. Thomas Evans (the best boss in the world) and Gus Krinakis (my favorite Greek) for their friendship and support through this process.

Writing a book must be a little like being pregnant. (Okay, not really, but bear with me.) From beginning to end, the process takes about nine months. You gain weight. And the end is much more stressful than the beginning. But the result is pretty special.

What you are holding in your hands is the result of nine months of a lot of hard work by a lot of people. We think she's pretty special.

Here's hoping you think so, too.